Going the Distance

Going the Distance

The College Athlete's Guide
to Excellence on the Field
and in the Classroom

Stephen K. Figler
Howard E. Figler

PETREL PRESS
P.O. Box 123
Placerville, CA 95667
(916) 621-0208

Peterson's Guides
Princeton, New Jersey

Library of Congress Cataloging-in-Publication Data

Figler, Stephen K.
    Going the distance : the college athlete's guide to excellence on
the field and in the classroom / Stephen K. Figler, Howard E. Figler.
        p.   cm.
    ISBN 0-87866-952-3
    1. College student orientation — United States. 2. College
athletes — United States. I. Figler, Howard E. II. Title.
LB2343.32.F54   1990
378.1'98 — dc20   90-43190

Composition and design by Peterson's Guides

Cover design by Greg Wuttke

Printed in the United States of America

10 9 8 7 6 5 4 3 2 1

Contents

Foreword

As graduation approaches each year, countless high school athletes naturally have high hopes of going on to intercollegiate competition. After entering college, many learn that they don't have enough talent. But for those who are blessed with exceptional athletic ability, there is an immediate challenge: how to handle the simultaneous pressures of competition in the classroom and on the playing field.

As statistics and news reports reveal, these pressures too often result in failure — academic, athletic, or both. Most of the tragedies can be averted if prospective student-athletes are properly prepared for the unique problems facing them and the extraordinary demands placed upon them.

I remember how hard it was for me to adjust during the first year I spent at Princeton University. When I was on the freshman basketball team, we practiced daily in the gym from about 4:30 p.m. until 7:30 at night. After the basketball season ended, I decided to play baseball, too. Halfway through that second semester, I discovered that my grades had dropped. Reluctantly, I gave up baseball and began going to the library every day, studying from 5 or 6 p.m. until midnight. By the end of the year, my grades had come up. That gave me great confidence. I knew then that I could compete in academics as well as athletics.

So I urge all college athletes to give top priority to getting the finest education that they can. That is their prime responsibility to themselves. Nothing is more important during their years in school, or for later success, and the sooner they know that, the better.

Similarly, student-athletes should have realistic expectations — recognizing that their future in sports is uncertain and that, even if they become professionals, life as a pro is short. Only 2 of every 100 college basketball players make it into the pros, and the average pro football career spans only three years.

Thus, it is essential for even the best college athletes to fully develop all their scholastic skills and prepare for life outside of sports. They must do their classwork with as much discipline and effort as they bring to athletic activities. For example, any basketball player who can concentrate inside a crowded arena and put in two game-winning foul shots can also study with intensity for a few hours each day. The trick is to use time well.

But student-athletes also should develop nonsports interests and be involved in various facets of campus life. This will help you to gain new experiences and the perspectives needed to make sound decisions.

Life is a series of choices. We have discretion in making those choices and in determining what we become.

As I was finishing high school, for instance, I was encouraged to go to a certain university and made plans to attend that school. But then I changed my mind and instead went to Princeton. When I earned my degree there, people advised me to play professional basketball. But I wanted some time to read, to study economics, to travel, and to gain perspective on myself and life. So I applied for a Rhodes Scholarship to go abroad to Oxford University. When I completed my studies there, people said I should attend law school. But I decided to play pro basketball. When my playing days ended ten years later, some people urged me to campaign for election to a position in local government. But I chose to run for a seat in the U.S. Senate.

The point is that all individuals have to decide what is best for themselves if they want to try to control their future. Because of the special abilities they have, athletes have many educational and career opportunities open to them.

Long before they go off to college, most athletes experience the satisfying feeling that comes from putting forth an effort in sports and succeeding. But if they are not ready to give as much for academic excellence by the time they enroll in college, they will not survive.

This is not a new problem. Everybody has heard about it. But it's not going away, and it may be getting worse instead of better.

By writing this book, Stephen and Howard Figler have made a major new attempt to focus attention on the situation. I hope that *Going the Distance* proves to be an important source of help to many student-athletes.

Bill Bradley
U.S. Senator, New Jersey
October 1990

Preface

In recent years a number of problems in college athletics have come to the public's attention. Among them are the following.

- The admission to college of academically unqualified student-athletes who must struggle to do college-level work.
- The funneling of athletes into "dummy" courses.
- Athletes' being required to spend so many hours at their sport that they have too few hours left for schoolwork.
- The low graduation rate of athletes, especially of those who are also members of minority groups.
- The payment of large salaries to a few star professional athletes while most pros struggle to make ends meet.
- The rules that make athletes pay for their coaches' athletics-related violations.
- Athletes' allowing others to do their academic and career planning for them, with the result that the athletes' education is undermined.
- The lack of participation by athletes in the areas of college life not related to sports.
- The use of steroids and other drugs by athletes at the expense of their health.

The National Collegiate Athletic Association (NCAA) and other associations that govern college athletics have been working to address these problems. The federal government, most notably through legislation sponsored by Senator Bill Bradley (D., New Jersey), is also trying to deal with the situation. Meanwhile, many state governments have enacted laws to deal with these issues, while some athletics conferences and individual schools have instituted their own testing procedures and rules.

Still, the problems listed above (there are others, too) persist for two reasons. First, college athletes often care so much about competing and succeeding in sports that they may overlook their own welfare (in the present as well as for the future). Second, coaches, athletics administrators, and fans care so much about winning that they too may overlook the welfare of the athletes. The bottom line is that if you want to "go the distance" in college and in your career after college, you must be aware of the hurdles and pitfalls that face you as an athlete. Take care of your own business; don't expect others to pave the way for you. In college, as in the rest of life, providence takes care of those who take care of themselves. *Going the Distance* is designed to help you do that.

To this revised edition of *The Athlete's Game Plan for College and Career* we have added three chapters directed toward specific areas of concern. Chapter 4, "Drugs and Sports," focuses on drug use by athletes. This chapter discusses steroids and other substances employed to improve performance as well as so-called "recreational" drugs. Chapter 5, "Special Considerations for Black Athletes," and Chapter 6, "Special Considerations for Women," deal with the special concerns of black and female athletes, respectively. Although the entire book is applicable to the concerns of these two groups, we believe that the special challenges that face female and black student-athletes are significant enough to warrant chapters of their own.

The purpose of *Going the Distance* is to enable every college athlete to achieve his or her goals equally well in sports, academics, and career preparation. In this book, we provide specific advice regarding how to balance these three areas of college life and solve the problems you will encounter in each of them. Student-athletes face pressures to neglect academics and career preparation in favor of sports involvement. *Going the Distance* will show you how to deal with these pressures and overcome them.

As educators, we can be accused of having a bias regarding the importance of higher education. It is, however, a bias borne of experience. Athletes who enter the work world with the ability to learn new skills, communicate effectively, and think creatively are far more likely to be promoted in their job, own their own business, and achieve success beyond the playing field. Often, athletes who short-circuit their education are unhappy, financially in debt, unable to advance or change their career, and, most of all, regretful that they did not complete their college degree.

We wrote this book because we believe that all student-athletes have unique qualities of leadership that they can offer, but only if they succeed in balancing sports and their education. Corporations and communities need the leadership of athletes: athletes' keen sense of teamwork, goal orientation, dedication to a task, and grace under pressure make them uniquely qualified to provide leadership for any kind of organization. The student-athlete who succeeds on the playing field *and* in the classroom will be an inspiration to anyone who must successfully balance competing priorities.

Stephen Figler
Howard Figler
October 1990

1

The Importance of Balance

The Problems of the Student-Athlete . . .
The ABCs of Being a Student-Athlete

The label of student-athlete says it all. A college student who is also an athlete is asked to live two roles and be two people in one. No other college students are identified in this hyphenated way — no others are pulled in two completely different directions. No other students are asked to be one person for half of the day and someone else for the other half. You don't hear college students referred to as student-actors, student–newspaper reporters, student–fraternity members, or student–computer jockeys. But being identified as a student-athlete is an acknowledgment that you are quite literally two beings, even though you have only one dormitory room, one body, and one mind to get both sets of tasks accomplished.

This dual role makes balance a crucial issue, for both your progress and your survival. How do you balance studies versus sports? How do you give equal attention to both without doing a disservice to either? Managing your time is a critical issue.

The amount of time athletes devote to their sport sets them apart from other students. While it's true that student government leaders, those who work on school publications, and those in drama or band also spend considerable time on activities, they seldom give the large number of hours for as many months as athletes do. Besides, they often can determine for themselves how much or how little time to devote to their activity, while athletes have no choice beyond the decision of whether or not to compete at all. Once an athlete decides to compete, the coach demands as much time of that athlete as the coach wants and needs.

College athletes often find they spend twice the amount of time training and competing in sports that they spent in high school, while at the same time, the amount of schoolwork has also doubled. This means the demands on your time in college are multiplied by four compared with high school. Managing your time is an even more difficult problem if your coach makes greater demands on your time — or if you make these demands on yourself.

College athletes are required to be full-time students progressing toward a degree. This is a full-time job and your primary responsibility. But in many cases the training, traveling, and competitive requirements of athletes cut into valuable study time. In order to handle both jobs — student and athlete — you must learn how to manage time extremely well — in fact, better than those who are only students.

Why should an athlete do two jobs instead of one?

> **You asked for it.** You are the one who wanted both a college degree and a career as an athlete. You'd be very disappointed if you had to give up athletics, so stay with it. Both sports and studies are rewarding. So, even though it may feel as if you are doing twice as much as the average college student, you're also getting twice the benefits and satisfactions.
>
> **Academics and athletics reinforce each other.** The same qualities that make you effective on the playing field will contribute toward your being a good student. Similarly, a well-organized and disciplined approach to studies will help you to concentrate better on the material you must learn for your sport.
>
> **The person who uses time well is usually more productive in every respect.** There's an old saying: If you want to get something done in a hurry, ask the busiest person in the room. The more you get done in a given week, the more efficient and productive you will tend to be overall. Success breeds success.

This book will show you that achieving a balance between athletics and academics is not only possible but also desirable. Your success as an athlete will help you as a student, and vice versa. What do we mean by balance? Balance is far more than just distributing your time to get all your tasks done and fulfill your responsibilities. Balance means:

1. Being equally committed to success in your sport and to the completion of your college degree. You won't be happy unless both goals are achieved with room to spare.
2. Using the same discipline and goal directedness in your academic work that you display toward your athletic goals. Your best qualities should be evident in everything you do.
3. Being just as responsible to the academic coach inside yourself as to the coach who directs your athletic efforts. Serving two masters isn't easy, but you don't want to disappoint either coach in any respect.

The last point is the hardest one to accomplish. Your sports coach may not want the same balance that you want between your academics and athletics. Nonetheless, you've got to figure out a way to avoid being overtaxed by your sport and to respond enthusiastically to your coach without neglecting your studies. Consider this: Experienced students are familiar with the concept of overstudying. They know it's possible to give *too much time* to a subject and thus perform more poorly. The same may apply to athletics. If you give your sport too much time, you may do *less well* than if you had struck a balance between it and the classroom. In the long run, balance will yield the best results on both sides of the fence.

The same qualities that make you effective on the playing field will contribute toward your being a good student.

All this sounds like one big pep talk. Fire up! Do both jobs! Don't let up! Wring the most out of yourself! It probably makes you tired just reading about it. Yes, we want your motivation to be as high as possible so that you have plenty to give to academics and athletics. And we are especially worried that you'll rob from your study time in an attempt to get an extra edge on the playing field. So, we push you to keep balance as a watchword. You'll do what you want to do anyway, but think of this pep talk every now and then when studies, grades, classes, and assignments seem the farthest thing from your mind. Give a nod to balance even when you don't want to. Why? Because when college is over we want you to say: "I'm thankful I gave enough to my studies that I now have a degree I can use, I have learning skills that will get me hired in a lot of jobs, and I am interested in something more in the world than just sports."

The Problems of the Student-Athlete

The athlete role brings with it certain problems that make it difficult to function as a regular student. Athletes' special problems, while largely invisible to the public and sometimes ignored by the college, are very real to athletes. We'll give brief explanations of some of these problems below. Later chapters consider these problems more fully and provide strategies and answers for dealing with them.

Eligibility

Every college student—athlete or not—must maintain a minimally acceptable grade point average to remain in good academic standing. The penalties for falling below that level are probation and, eventually, disqualification from school if the deficient GPA is not corrected. Also, students on an athletics scholarship or grant must take a certain minimum number of units to be eligible to participate in team play. These are only two of the many eligibility rules that athletes must concern themselves with.

Coaches have been known to suggest—and even to order—athletes to take only the minimum units needed to remain eligible. This leaves more time for athletics and team commitments, but it makes the eligibility issue a constant problem for many athletes. As an athlete, you might be tempted to take the least difficult or most convenient minimum number of course hours you can find rather than challenge yourself with more substantial and meaningful classes. Focusing on minimum eligibility instead of on academic progress toward a degree can detract from the quality of your education and lead to unforeseen problems when graduation finally does draw near.

4

Financial Problems

College athletes often have special financial needs, not because they require any more money than nonathletes but because they rarely have the time, much less the energy, to earn money from a part-time job. It's tough enough to do well in two full-time jobs (sports and academics) without adding a part-time job.

Many athletes receive an athletics grant, an academic scholarship, or a loan or grant based on need. But even the best financial aid package is designed to cover only basic educational and living expenses. Little, if anything, is left over for daily expenses, clothes, and entertainment. Sports boosters, and even coaches, may offer to help athletes with their financial difficulties, and the athlete presented with such offers may be tempted to accept the extra aid. But doing so can lead to far more serious problems, such as loss of amateur standing and penalties to the school's athletics program.

Personal Pressures

Coaches and teammates exert pressure on you to be committed and to do well in your sport. Pressure also may come from fans and boosters. In some sports, the media bring added pressure. Even when your particular public — your group of fans — is small and the press couldn't care less, you're likely to feel some pressure to please them. But the most consistent source of pressure on college athletes comes from within themselves. Even when athletes have done well personally, they often feel they bear some guilt if the team doesn't win. They feel there is always something more they could have done to bring victory. This is a special pressure known to all athletes but felt by very few outside of sports.

Academic Progress

It may seem strange to single out athletes as having problems in making academic progress. Isn't it a problem for all students? It is, but the problem takes on special dimensions for athletes. Identifying a major field of study and maintaining progress toward a degree are two sides of the same need: gaining an interesting and useful education. In addition to the personal and time pressures just discussed, some people believe that athletes aren't suited to some majors. This may lead athletes who haven't yet identified a field of study to select an easier major than they otherwise might choose, or simply to pick one (such as physical education or recreation) that is often identified with athletes.

Athletes may eliminate a preferred major and career direction because it conflicts with the sports side of their life. Or, they might proceed toward a degree at a slower pace than other students — because of athletic commitments. None of these problems relating to academic progress necessarily results from being a college athlete, yet the fact that each occurs illustrates the need athletes have for special guidance.

Career Selection

The intensity with which college athletes compete in their sport and the consuming part it plays in their lives inhibit many athletes from planning for life after college. Too often, athletes don't take the time and effort to do any active, future-oriented career planning. Why struggle with the future when the present is so much fun and so rewarding? And, of course, there are many college athletes whose planning for the future begins and ends with their dreams of a career in professional sports.

[Some college officials] think of their athletes as if they were disposable razor blades. They give them uniforms, schedule games for them, and sell tickets so they can make money and paint their gym or buy nice new desks for the athletic department, and when the kids are used up they simply throw them away, with no conscience. . . . The world is full of people who are only too ready to think you're a fool, just because you're a jock.

Comments of a news editor who covers college sports [1]

The ABCs of Being a Student-Athlete

The foregoing problems and others like them can be avoided only if you look upon your college years as an integrated package of athletics, education, and career preparation. Problems often occur because athletes allow their sport to dominate them to the detriment of their education and career. We call looking at the overall picture of your life in college the ABCs of being a student-athlete.

A Is for Athlete

Not only do college athletes *want* to compete, but they also have a *need* to compete. They often are willing to sacrifice what nonathletes take for granted: leisure time, extra money from a part-time job, a full social life, a body free from pain, time for studies, and privacy. Competing in their sport is more important to athletes than any or all of these other aspects of college life. Many athletes don't even weigh the value of competing on a team against the loss of these other things. No contest! This is often as true of the small-college athlete in a minor sport as it is of the big-time football or basketball player. We are describing *desire* — the desire of a person to compete and be known as an athlete. The desire to be an athlete may be the single most important motivation currently in your life.

Although college athletes give up much of what other students take for granted, they receive a lot in return. In addition to the sheer pleasure of competing, athletes often gain respect and adulation, a strong and attractive body, the opportunity to travel, practice in operating under pressure, helpful personal contacts, the possibility of fame, and even a slim chance at fortune. In other words, participation in athletics can enrich your life immensely and you can have a heck of a good time in the process.

B Is for Other Benefits College Can Bring

The important benefits of your years in college are *not* only the credits and grades you get on a transcript. Real and meaningful benefits come from the things you do in the classroom, your discussions with other students between classes, your efforts and accomplishments outside of the classroom in addition to athletics, your interaction with faculty and college staff, your development of good reading and study habits and the skill of critical thinking, and your gaining an appreciation for knowledge and what it can do.

You may find ways of getting good grades and piling up credits in easy courses without really learning much of value. (Even the best schools have Mickey Mouse courses.) But earning credits that way is like winning an athletic contest against a poor, underpowered opponent; there isn't much value or satisfaction in it. In fact, it's a waste of your time and effort compared with what you could be doing. The choice is yours: you can miss out on most of the potential for learning and personal growth simply by doing only what is necessary to stay eligible for sports, or you can take the more rewarding road and try to get all of the benefits that college has to offer.

Coaches often point out that how you practice is how you will play, meaning that practice is the time for building good habits that can be called on during the pressure of competition. Habits built in schoolwork carry into athletics, and habits built in athletics should carry into schoolwork. Athletes who get into the habit of taking the easy way in schoolwork will probably do the same in athletics. They may be able to fool the coach, but their teammates know who isn't going all out.

The direct and indirect benefits of college can, if you let them, take you far beyond what is gained by being just an athlete. These benefits include:

- Development or improvement of work habits
- Practice and direction in solving problems
- Development of the ability to think critically and make informed decisions
- Broader knowledge and appreciation of the world
- Greater understanding of your place in the world
- Knowledge of specific new subjects
- Useful and enjoyable lifelong personal contacts
- An interesting career direction

These are the best fruits of a college education, and all college students, including athletes, should have all of them when they graduate. You shouldn't be satisfied with less.

C Is for the Career You Are Approaching

In some cases, depending on your major, a college education can lead you directly into a career. Engineering, computer science, and accounting are some popular examples. With other majors, the education cultivates universal skills that you may then have to mold into a career in your own way. English, history, mathematics, and psychology are some examples. But in all cases, your experience in college should help you grow to the point where a career of your choosing is within reach. This obviously won't be the case if you spend your years in college as an "eligibility major" — someone who takes only enough units to stay eligible for sports.

Your initial career choice may have something to do with your experience and interest in sports. But the choice you ultimately make will more than likely be influenced by your other skills, interests, and nonsports experiences. The combination of what you gain from sports and what you learn from schoolwork and the other aspects of college life should give you more skills and broadened contacts and interests, so that you are more likely to make a wise and informed career choice.

Remember the ABCs of the college athlete's life. You are best served — now and in the long run — by taking care of each of the three concerns. Coaches, fans, and even some teammates may want you to emphasize athletics at the expense of the full benefits of a college education and your future career. At colleges where athletics are at odds with these other concerns, athletes are being exploited. You are the best one — at some schools, the only one — to make sure that you aren't exploited. You should gain more from college than just a few years as an athlete. You deserve more lasting benefits from your college education, and you deserve a healthy start toward an interesting, worthwhile career.

A diet of easy courses means you've lost out on a worthwhile education.

Don't expect college to provide these benefits automatically. College officials — coaches, professors, advisers, and counselors — may not follow the progress of your education very closely. (Eligibility, yes; progress, no.) They may claim in public that they care about how well their athletes do in the classroom, and they may even monitor your progress toward graduation, but you can't count on these individuals to know or care whether you are learning very much that will help in your life after college.

A diet of easy courses means you've lost out on a worthwhile education. When you cannot get or hold a decent job because you cannot communicate effectively or solve problems efficiently, the employer will not be sympathetic to the excuse that you were busy being an athlete in college.

Does a degree mean that you are educated? A combination of academic concessions, easy courses, and low grading standards for athletes could mean that you might accumulate enough credits to receive a college degree but doesn't mean that you have learned anything of value in the process. It's up to you to *earn* your education. Once you receive an empty education, it will be far harder to obtain a useful one. Other colleges may not want you. Besides, you'll probably be tired of being a student by then. We want you to get a high-quality education now, while the getting is still good.

The ABCs are the basic and most important elements of the athlete's years in college. If you leave college having had a good athletics experience, having earned a good and useful education, and with a promising career direction in mind, you've done well, and the college has done well by you. If you miss out on one or two of these elements, you've been cheated — or you've cheated yourself.

One of the hardest things that any athlete has to face is the end of his or her career in active, high-level competition. The trip from star status to has-been takes only a moment. Many former athletes have called it a kind of death. The best way to beat that death is to prepare for a life after athletics and college. You, the athlete, can prepare for your life in the work world by paying attention to your schoolwork and career development while you're in college living it up as an athlete. That first step beyond college is a long and steep one, and there are far fewer people around willing to help a former athlete than there were in the days when that same person had eligibility remaining.

Because the pressures on an athlete to perform are so enormous, a high-quality education may elude you unless you learn how to make the system work in your favor. You've got to strive to be successful in both sides of your student-athlete role, despite the many obstacles you'll face. This book identifies those obstacles and offers solutions to help you have a good athletic experience while obtaining the education that will benefit you in your career and throughout your life.

2

Getting Along with Coaches, Boosters, Professors, and Others

The Athlete and the Coach . . . The Athlete and Boosters . . . The Athlete and the College Administration . . . The Athlete and the Faculty . . . The Athlete and Other Students . . . The Athlete and Gamblers

Student-athletes often have a different relationship with other members of the campus community from that of nonathletes. To the extent that they are identified as athletes, people tend to relate to them as athletes first and students second — or in some cases, as athletes only. Athletes also sometimes attract the attention of fans, boosters, and sportswriters, none of whom have an official function on the college campus. Understanding these interpersonal relationships and the expectations people may have of you as an athlete will help you to get along better in college and will keep you from making some serious mistakes.

The Athlete and the Coach

It doesn't take a genius to know that in sports, for every winner there is at least one loser. In track and field, gymnastics, swimming, and other sports where more than two teams compete together, there is one winner and there are several losers. And if a particular team is expected to win a championship, its members can be considered losers — even with a winning record — if they

11

fall short of their championship goal. (The coaching graveyard is full of those who earned winning records but not enough championships.)

Most coaches feel some pressure to win, whether the pressure comes from others or is self-imposed. These two factors — that coaches are expected to win and everyone cannot always win — help to explain why few coaches keep the same job or stay in the profession of coaching for very many years. Those who consistently lose usually are fired or quit; those who win and are ambitious (as coaches tend to be) move on to bigger challenges.

No matter how good a strategist, how well organized, or how skillful a psychologist, a coach will not win consistently without good athletes. But many coaches feel that having good athletes (resulting from luck or recruiting effort) is not even enough to help them become and stay winners. They also need *commitment* to the sport from their athletes. Some coaches simply ask their athletes for this commitment — others demand it. What does this commitment mean to you as a student-athlete?

The Time Problem

Commitment to athletics is most apparent in terms of time and energy devoted to training and to the team. As a college athlete you can expect to spend 25 to 50 or more hours each week in your sport. Coaches generally expect the hours required for team-related tasks (practices, travel, games, conditioning, chalk-talks, etc.) to be taken from your leisure time, which they often consider a low priority. This is part of the price athletes are expected to pay for the privilege of playing for the college. But everybody wants and needs a certain amount of leisure and personal time. Since no one has yet found more than 24 hours in a day, college athletes often have to steal the time required for team-related tasks from somewhere else. Instead of sacrificing their leisure time, they usually end up sacrificing schoolwork or sleep.

Jeff Hembrough, formerly a tackle on the Illinois State University football team who majored in chemistry, was honored in 1981 by the Football Foundation and Hall of Fame as an All-America Scholar-Athlete. Hembrough describes the time problem facing most college athletes:

> We devoted more than 40 hours a week to football. It's almost like having a full-time job and then having to do schoolwork. For the poor student, this is tough. He needs more time, and when he

gets in trouble academically, it is harder for him to find the time as he falls behind.[1]

Since no one has yet found more than 24 hours in a day, college athletes often have to steal the time for team-related tasks from somewhere else. Instead of sacrificing leisure time, they usually end up sacrificing schoolwork or sleep.

Winning Versus Your Welfare

Coaches feel that the time commitment they demand of athletes is necessary in order to have a winning team. Most coaches are also genuinely concerned about the personal and academic welfare of their athletes. Unfortunately, when the welfare of their athletes conflicts with the chance to win, there are too many coaches who will sacrifice the former for the latter. If you find yourself working with a coach for whom your personal welfare is little more than an afterthought, especially if your health or academic progress is suffering because of the coach's demands, you should seriously consider either transferring to another school or quitting the team. Those are drastic measures, but the consequences of staying in a bad environment and wasting your education are worse.

What Do You Want from Your Coach?

Athletes learn early to figure out what the coach wants from them but seldom try to determine, beyond the obvious, what they want and should get from the coach. First, all athletes want the coach to allow them to compete. Next, they want the coach to teach new techniques and strategies and correct their faults. A college coach should also be a good counselor and guide and not a dictator or guardian figure who takes care of everything. "Taking care of everything" usually means taking most of your choices away from you (including the selection of classes, whom you'll live with, and where you'll get a part-time or summer job). Having someone make decisions for you is *not* what college is sup-

posed to be about; that encourages dependence, which can crip-
ple you when you have to act on your own. What you want from
your coach is for him or her to allow you to make your own
academic and career decisions and to support them with good
information and counsel. In the long run, your coach's interest in
your progress in areas other than athletics will be the most lasting
benefit the coach can give you.

Dealing with the Coach's Personality

You may like your coach's personality or you may hate it, but
you have to deal with it if you want to be allowed to compete. As
any athlete knows all too well, the coach holds power over one of
the most important concerns in your life: your access to competing.

Since coaches have ultimate power over who gets to compete,
dealing with their personalities generally means adjusting to
them rather than having them adjust to you. Some coaches are
unemotional and distant from their athletes. Others project a
warm and parentlike or buddy image to their athletes. Still others
present themselves as antagonists, always seeming to dig at their
athletes, criticizing and harping on the most minor errors and
keeping everyone on edge. Everyone has a different coaching
style.

Whichever face your coach wears, it's probably one that he or
she feels will work most effectively to produce a successful team.
The "coaching face" — the way coaches treat and interact with
their athletes — is usually a means for motivating and controlling
athletes.

Many coaches either can't or won't treat each of their athletes as
individuals with different needs. If you don't like the way your
coach is treating you, it's your responsibility to do something
about it. If you think that your coach has the wrong image of you,
your choice is either to suffer along with the old image or take the
initiative to correct that image and establish a new relationship
with the coach. Don't expect the coach to take the lead — he or she
has a lot of athletes to deal with.

Changing the way you relate to people isn't easy. But don't
mistakenly believe that the way you've related to coaches or
teammates in the past is the way you must continue to act. You
always have the ability to change your image. If, for example, you

14

have become the team clown but want to be taken more seriously, it's up to you to change that image. Since the coach often influences the roles people play on their team, let the coach know that you would prefer to be taken more seriously.

In the long run, your coach's interest in your progress in areas other than athletics will be the most lasting benefit the coach can give you.

Coaches will often respond well to this kind of direct approach. It generates respect as a mature way of dealing with a conflict between two people who have to work closely together. Some coaches, on the other hand, will react poorly to an athlete who tries to correct the coach's mistaken image and establish a better relationship. Trying to improve the coach's image of you may seem like a gamble, but in the long run it will be worth the risk. It's better than spending a few years not getting along with the coach, hanging onto the futile hope that something will change the situation for you. That something often takes the form of a dream that a chance will come for you to prove yourself by winning a big contest for the coach. The chance of that happening is not likely if you and your coach don't get along.

The Athlete and Boosters

Who are college athletics boosters? Most people assume that athletics boosters are alumni of the college and, conversely, that all alumni are athletics boosters. In reality, many graduates of a college do not actively support the school's teams. Many don't even like sports. Many athletics boosters are simply fans who have affiliated themselves with a particular college, even though they have never taken a class at the school. Their interest in the college lies in having a team to root for.

The quote from SMU athletics director Bob Hitch that appears on page 17 foreshadowed the death penalty that SMU's football program received in 1987 from the NCAA, which disallowed its participation in college football for a two-year period. Boosters invariably appear to athletes as friends, even though they often do more harm to athletes and entire athletics programs than an enemy ever could. The recent probations suffered by the SMU, Texas A&M, and University of Florida football teams are only a few of the many that resulted from overzealous booster involvement. In fact, in the 1980s, *nearly half* of all of the Division I schools were put on probation by the NCAA.

Harm to athletes and programs occurs because boosters want so badly for the athletics program to be successful. Many boosters feel that success in sports is worth any price. Yet they often seem ignorant of (or unwilling to accept) the fact that tactics that may have led to success in their own businesses and professions are either inappropriate or illegal in college athletics.

Question: Why are athletics boosters interested in you?

Answer: Because of your athletic ability and, in particular, what you can do for the team.

Question: What can you do for the team if you suffer a disabling injury or use up your playing ability?

Answer: Nothing!

Question: What interest are boosters likely to have in you if you become injured or after your college athletic career is over?

Answer: Considerably less than when you were an active member of the team. You weren't the first athlete they befriended, and you won't be the last. There is always someone new coming along on whom boosters can lavish their attention, money, and advice.

Be friendly with athletics boosters, especially if they are friendly to you. But also be wary of them. The history of college sports is filled with incidents where something has gone wrong in the relationship among athletes, teams, and boosters. The problem usually arises when boosters want to help too much and so offer more to individual athletes than the rules allow. Not long ago, the University of San Francisco decided to drop its entire men's intercollegiate basketball program because of excessive booster involvement. The University's administrators reinstated the team only when they felt confident that they could control boosters.

What sort of help do boosters frequently attempt to make available to athletes? The following are typical.

Money: from pocket change to thousands of dollars or use of credit cards. (Even the pocket change is illegal.)

Gifts: from "a little something from the store" to cars, trips, and even houses. (All gifts to athletes are illegal, except gifts from their own family.)

Advice: from game strategy to opinions about majors and careers. (There are better sources to get advice from than boosters.)

Contacts: with people who can help athletes get started in careers once their college days end. (Career contacts are important and the best legitimate benefit that boosters can offer.)

Clearly, some athletes don't care about getting an education and willingly sell themselves to the highest bidder. Also, many coaches are interested only in building a winning team any way they can. Even college presidents have been known to look the other way when rules have been broken, and some welcome the involvement and largess of wealthy boosters. Ironically, without the boosters' intense interest in being associated with winning athletic teams, many of the temptations some student-athletes face (Should you take the money? Are you a fool if you don't take it?) would not exist.

People in the business world [sports boosters] are not always interested in the rules and regulations [of college athletics]—they feel they know how to make a sale. We do our best to monitor their activities, but it isn't easy.

Bob Hitch, athletics director at
Southern Methodist University [2]

Most boosters mean well. The problem lies with those boosters who fail to understand the difficult — and potentially damaging — position they put athletes in by offering them illegal bonuses. Boosters may not want to consider the ethical problems they create for you. Having their team win may be, to them, considerably more important than following the rules. Besides, the rules and penalties apply to you, the athlete, not to them. They have nothing to lose; it's you and your team who will pay the price.

In addition to being harmful to student-athletes and their colleges, the booster activities described in this section are illegal. New NCAA rules attempt to prevent boosters from contacting and influencing student-athletes, but they are likely to find ways around the rules — they always have.

The Athlete and the College Administration

If athletics programs are so costly and cause so much trouble, why do colleges have them? The answer is that college administrators believe at least one and probably all of the following:

- An athletics program earns money for the college.
- An athletics program is entertaining and attracts students to the college.
- An athletics program provides good public relations for the college.
- An athletics program gives students, faculty, and staff a sense of identity with the college.
- An athletics program keeps alumni interested in the college and thus ensures a major source of ongoing contributions to the college.
- An athletics program provides the kind of learning experience that can't be found in the classroom.

Further, many college administrators believe that if athletics bring these things to their school, then a winning athletics program, particularly in the mass-audience sports of football and basketball, will do even more.

It's not enough just to know that your school's administration supports the athletics program. You should also understand what it expects of your coach, since one way or another you will feel the expectations that your coach labors under. It is often the school's administration that demands winning teams and thus inadvertently sets the ball rolling toward cheating on rules and exploitation of athletes. In situations where administrators, boosters, and coaches are all committed to winning (a favorite phrase), an even greater commitment is expected of the athletes themselves. As a result, student-athletes may have even greater difficulty finding enough time and energy to take care of their education and career needs.

The greater the expectations and pressure to win placed upon your coach by the college administration, the greater the expectations and pressure your coach will place on you. When an expectation becomes a demand for success, people often feel pressured to change their attitudes and behaviors to support that demand at the expense of other needs. A coach who initially seemed friendly and relaxed may become distant and tense. A coach who had always seemed concerned for your welfare may ask you to play when you are injured. A coach who previously seemed concerned about your future might suggest you take a light or easy class load if difficult courses are diverting your attention from the team. Athletes who find themselves caught in that trap must have the courage to resist pressure from coaches to neglect their academic goals.

The Athlete and the Faculty

On any campus, some professors have a reputation for being proathletics, while others are known as antijock. You cannot tell if professors are proathletics or antiathletics by whether or not they were athletes during their high school and college days. Some former athletes are extremely antiathletics, particularly regarding the way sports are conducted in colleges. Conversely, many professors who were not athletes themselves are among the strongest backers of athletics.

Nearly every college has a few professors who dislike athletics so much that they are unfair to athletes. They group athletes into one or two categories, usually labeled "dumb" and "pampered." These professors are biased, and their minds are usually closed to any evidence to the contrary about athletes. Avoid taking classes from these antiathletics professors whenever possible, unless you have a large margin for error in your GPA and feel like being a crusader for athletes' rights. Why make college life any harder than it has to be? If you can't avoid them, keep a low profile concerning your involvement in athletics. Try not to ask for favors (alternative test dates, delayed assignments, etc.) because of team commitments, avoid responding to questions or commenting on assignments in terms of your experience in sports, and certainly don't wear your practice jersey to class.

G**o out of your way to communicate to every one of your teachers that you are a serious student.**

Some simple techniques can be followed that will help you get along with faculty members no matter what their attitudes toward athletes. These techniques are not intended just to impress professors; they will make you a better student. One of the most obvious techniques is to pay attention in class. You'd be surprised how easily professors can identify students who are paying attention and how much they like those who do. When professors ask a question in class, they usually would like a response from the students rather than to have to answer the question themselves. Don't worry about giving the wrong answer. An erroneous yet thoughtful response that indicates you have been paying attention is almost as good as the correct answer. In some cases a thoughtful wrong answer is *better than* the right answer, because it allows the professor to then explain his or her intention for asking the question in the first place.

You can establish your credibility as a student by being on time to classes and meetings and demonstrating the other qualities that professors associate with good students. Specifically,

- Turn in assignments on time or early.
- Prepare early for tests. Most professors can tell when a student has waited until the last night to study, and they aren't likely to be sympathetic to excuses.

- Ask to take tests early when you know there will be a schedule conflict because of your sport. Your best bet is to talk about this the first week of the term by bringing the team schedule to your professors to discuss the conflicts with them. They will appreciate your foresight and concern. Few things irritate professors more than to have an athlete (or anyone) come to them after missing a test and ask for a make-up exam.

- Meet with professors early in the term (or even before it starts) and ask their advice about what is needed to do well in the course. Professors are used to athletes' asking for special favors to get around course requirements, so you will be well received if, instead, you ask *how to do well* in the class.

A must-do investment of time for you during your hours away from athletics is to meet individually with your faculty members. Developing positive relationships with faculty is very important in ensuring your progress as a student and the completion of your degree. This doesn't mean brownnosing. It means going out of your way to communicate to every one of your teachers that you are a serious student who is committed to receiving a high-quality education. Your task is to work with your professors toward that end.

The Athlete and Other Students

Getting Along with Nonathletes

As do professors, nonathletes come in three varieties: those who are proathletics, those who are antiathletics, and those who couldn't care less. In college as compared with high school, the extremes of either loving or hating athletics are further apart. College students who love athletics are more likely to be in awe of athletes (this tendency is greater in college than in high school possibly because athletic skill tends to be greater at the college level). On the other hand, college students who dislike athletics are likely to be more active and vocal in their feelings. This may affect you in social situations and in classes. An antiathletic feeling may even hurt your team financially on campuses where funding for athletics comes in part from student government.

Many nonathletes have their own expectations of what athletes are like and how they are supposed to act. Those who think that athletes are dumb, aggressive, or not serious about school may cause a problem for you. Student-athletes may feel tension when they are expected to be smart in their role as a college student and dumb in their role as a jock. Role conflict has burdened many athletes from the early history of college sports. The dumb-jock image has been well earned by some athletes and as a result, that stereotype has had to be battled by most other athletes. Relate to nonathlete students as equals. Be as smart as you know you are. Don't live down to some image they may have about athletes. Be yourself. That will be good enough for anyone.

Don't Limit Yourself to Athletes as Companions

Don't let the special bond that exists among athletes become a shackle on your social interactions and cause you to associate only with other athletes. Up to this point in your life, you may have been most comfortable in the company of other athletes, but after you graduate, there will no longer be the same kind of distinction between athletes and nonathletes. If you haven't already done so, now is the time to become comfortable with nonathletes and build relationships on other interests.

Some athletes you know, especially those who are unsure of themselves, may try to put you down for associating with nonathletes. This response reflects their weakness, not yours. The more you hang around only with other athletes, the more likely you are to think of college (and maybe even life) primarily in athletic terms.

The Athlete and Gamblers

A discussion of how an athlete can get along in college is not complete without considering how you can and should handle gamblers.[3] It would be nice not to have to concern ourselves with this problem, yet the gambling scandals in the 1980s at Tulane University and Boston College show how real the problem is. The playing career of former Ohio State University quarterback Art Schlichter was ruined by a gambling habit, while the legendary status of professional baseball's Pete Rose was shattered in the same way.

Football and basketball players tend to be more attractive to gamblers than athletes from other sports. But not all gambling is on major contests of national interest. Local gamblers have their own systems and networks for small colleges. Gamblers have been known to bet on snail races, so no athlete should assume that he or she is immune to this problem.

Let's say that a gambler, or even a teammate, approaches you to keep the score close — not to lose the contest, but just to shave enough points off the final score so that gamblers can beat the point spread and win their bets. You are offered a few hundred dollars in cash to take it easy if it looks as though your team is going to beat the point spread.

The money being offered to you may seem like a lot at the time, especially if you really need it. But in the long run the few hundred or even thousand dollars you make from gamblers would be meaningless next to what it could cost you, your teammates and coach, and the school. Games, championships, and careers have been lost to involvement with gamblers.

They will try to make you believe that by shaving points you aren't doing anything too terrible. You might even fool yourself into thinking that you're hurting only people who are breaking the law by betting with the gamblers. But consider the following:

1. Shaving points is illegal and punishable.

2. Not trying your hardest in any contest is unethical.

3. Not even the best players can control a contest well enough to determine the final score. Many contests have been lost that were just supposed to be kept close.

Being approached by a gambler is a little like getting hit by a truck. You didn't ask for the problem, but you can't ignore it. Tell your coach about any contact you have had with a gambler or with someone you think might be a gambler. Don't mistakenly think that you can keep clean by keeping quiet. The rules of collegiate athletics state that you are as guilty by remaining quiet as you are if you participate. Gamblers know that in keeping silent you have broken a rule, and they will use that knowledge to draw you further into their web by attempting to involve you in point-shaving schemes or in throwing a contest. It will probably be hard for you to report the contact to your coach, especially if the contact involves a teammate. But the consequences of not doing it are worse.

3

Getting Your Questions Answered

*Is It a Rule, or Do You Have a Choice? . . .
Official Advisers . . . Special Advising Programs
for Athletes . . . Unofficial Advisers . . . Special
Organizations That Help Athletes*

When you need advice about your college education, there are places to get official advice and counseling. Official advice comes from people who have been hired by the college specifically to counsel and communicate information to students. Unofficial advice comes from anywhere else. Although finding official sources of advice may take a little effort on your part, the effort is usually worth the trouble. The advice and counseling you get from these official sources are more sound and consistent than any you might get through unofficial sources, such as alumni, coaches, or the student grapevine.

Students who take full advantage of advisers and counselors consistently do better in their classwork and are more likely to graduate. Your willingness to work with advisers is a good measure of your commitment to your academic program. Staying in regular contact with your advisers will enable you to avoid making mistakes that will keep you from graduating. Advisers exist to answer all of your questions. If you can't get the information you need from one adviser, seek another one until you have everything you need to know.

Is It a Rule, or Do You Have a Choice?

There is a difference between matters of school policy — rules — and matters of choice. Policies and rules are published in the college catalog and other official publications. Although you are responsible for knowing the rules, official school advisers should help you interpret them. Advisers can also give you advice on matters of choice, such as which courses will best serve your needs. But in these matters of choice, you should not look for *answers* from other people. In general, there is no single right answer in matters of choice. Instead, several good options usually exist, from which you have to select the best one for your situation.

Advisers help keep you on track toward your degree, making sure you are completing the required courses. They also help you to consider how to manage your time. Perhaps their best form of help is to ask questions that make you consider what your priorities are.

What sort of advice or counseling do you need? You need or will need advice about how to acquire a solid education and a useful degree, how to make the most of your college athletic career, and how and where to look toward a career outside of athletics. The following sources should help you when you need information, advice about problems, and help with decision making.

Official Advisers

Professors

Professors often act as advisers to students, explaining academic requirements and other information contained in the official college catalog. You will either be assigned to a professor when you enter the college or be allowed to choose one from the faculty in your major department. Your academic adviser should help you in developing your academic program, selecting courses each term, and fulfilling your degree requirements in the major.

Just as with coaches, some professors are better advisers than others. Professors are seldom trained as advisers and often are not paid for it. They are trained, hired, paid, and judged on the teaching and research they do. Advising students is a task that comes out of time they might prefer to use doing other things. Some enjoy advising and put a lot of effort into it; others don't. Look for one who seems to care about advising and about you. How can you tell how much care and effort faculty members put into advising? Ask yourself the following questions:

- Do they know the rules, regulations, deadlines, and so on?

- If not, are they willing to help you find out this important information?

- Are they willing to spend some time with you exploring your interests, or do you get the feeling that they are rushing you through the advising session?

- Do they simply *tell you* what to take, without exploring your own interests and alternative ways of approaching your degree and career goals?

Getting good advice and counsel from faculty members is very important. If the professor assigned to you (or chosen by you) for advising isn't doing well for you, either talk to him or her about it or look around for someone who might give you better advising service.

The rewards for collegiate athletic participation are dismal . . . for those who are not fortunate enough to have proper guidance or counseling during their undergraduate career. They could end up majoring in courses to no-man's land. Too many athletes are hopeless cases without a chance of a pro sports career or a degree — after sacrificing four or five years, all at a loss.

Oscar Edwards, former UCLA football player [1]

You want an adviser who will tell you how your education relates to life after college. There are enough other people around to help you become eligible or stay eligible for sports. Some schools have lists of mentors who have volunteered to give more personal advice. Check at the student services center or campus counseling office.

Student Services

Academic advising center. Some colleges and universities, especially large ones, have special offices for advising students on academic matters. This service is offered in addition to the departmental adviser to whom you will be assigned in your major. You can expect to find out information about general requirements for graduation, and your progress can be monitored at such an office. You may also get help with major requirements at the academic advising center. Often, a member of its staff will serve as your official adviser until you select a major.

In addition to advice on degree requirements, the academic advising staff can explain the grading system, help you figure out your GPA, and discuss changing majors or even transferring to another school. They do not do career counseling. Their task is to provide you with help in getting the most out of what college has to offer — in particular, a degree.

No matter what any adviser tells you, even those in the college advising center, the responsibility for your actions rests on your shoulders alone. If you don't double-check advice and it turns out to be wrong, you're likely to spend extra time and effort making up for the mistake. Be like a bulldog about making sure you have good information; it's your education and future on the line.

Learning skills center. In the learning skills center you will find tutors, workshops, self-instruction programs, and other help in improving the skills essential to learning. Typical workshops deal with improving reading and writing, test-taking, time management, listening and note-taking, and memory enhancement.

Testing center. In the testing center, you may take exams for remedial help or advanced placement (reading, writing, math, etc.) or for identification of your interests (such as the Strong-Campbell Interest Inventory). Tests for graduate school admission, such as the Graduate Record Examinations and the Miller Analogies Test, may also be offered. Some schools combine the testing center and learning skills center.

Health center. At the campus health center, you can get medical help and may be able to take the preseason physical exams required by your sport.

Psychological counseling center. You can receive help with stress and other personal problems in the psychological counseling center. Many small colleges combine psychological and career counseling in one office; some schools place psychological counseling in the health center.

Career development and placement center. Most colleges have a special office or center for counseling students about their career interests and career alternatives. If your school has a career development and placement center, check into what it offers. Don't wait until you are about to graduate to seek help from the career center. Career advice can be helpful to you as early as your first year in college.

Student employment office. You can locate part-time jobs and summer jobs, either on or off campus, in the student employment office. Don't confuse the student employment office with the career center. (The former deals with your job needs while you are a student; the latter helps you find a career direction and learn the right way to search for a position in your field.)

Educational Opportunity Program (EOP). If you are from an economically disadvantaged background, you can get help through EOP with special admissions (if you don't meet the normal school entrance requirements), counseling to help you adjust to the college environment, special tutors in basic communication and math skills, and small grants (between $200 and $1,000) to help you through the school year.

Financial aid office. The financial aid office exists to help you determine the amount of aid you need and to help you find appropriate sources of this aid. Your coach may help set up your initial contact with the financial aid office, but don't wait for this to happen. Every coach has his or her personal view of how much initiative student-athletes should take in obtaining financial aid.

The financial aid office may have someone who specializes in helping athletes, but again, don't count on it. Even if the financial aid office has such a specialist, don't expect this person to come to you or to drop everything else when you walk in the door. Financial aid offices are very busy places. At some colleges, more than 80 percent of the students receive some sort of aid. Bear in mind that all aid recipients must apply through the same office. A lesson you should have learned in sports applies also to seeking financial aid: "Persistence pays off!"

Unless you have either a full or partial athletics scholarship, you will probably be just like any other student to those who work in the financial aid office. Even if they tend to treat athletes in some special way, you'll be doing yourself a favor not to expect special treatment.

Large colleges tend to have separate offices for each of the student services just mentioned, while smaller schools may combine the services into one or two offices. A final and very important comment on student services: you must approach them — they won't be likely to come looking for you. If you need any of these services, don't be bashful about seeking them out. They exist to help all students, including athletes.

Students who want and need financial aid must keep the appointments they make, they must follow through on what they start, and above all, they must be persistent. Don't be shy about coming back time and again to check that your file is in order and to see what's available. We won't get tired of seeing you.

Kathy Blattner, financial aid officer
California State University, Sacramento

Special Advising Programs for Athletes

A growing number of colleges have one or more advisers whose job is to work with athletes. These specialists provide advice and counsel about many concerns, including monitoring eligibility for competition. About half of the universities in Division I of the NCAA employ at least one adviser or counselor especially for athletes. In Divisions II and III of the NCAA, about one college in nine has a special adviser for athletes. If your school has a special adviser or counselor for athletes, that person will focus on helping you progress with normal speed toward a degree, select or change majors, find a career direction, and deal with other matters of concern in the life of a college student.

Your college may even have an extensive support program for athletes that gives them a special orientation before their first semester, administers placement or diagnostic tests, operates a tutoring program and/or study tables for athletes, and provides what is normally thought of as academic advising—identifying courses, explaining graduation requirements, helping with the choice of a major, and so on. This support program may also conduct stress counseling, run study skills workshops, bring people onto campus to describe various careers, and even serve as a link to professors on campus. About 200 universities and colleges across the nation currently offer a special support program for athletes, and the number is growing.

In spite of this trend, many colleges don't have enough money to hire a special counselor, much less to fund an entire support program for athletes. Or, they may see their athletes as not so different from other students that they need a special adviser. Consider it a plus if a school has a special advising program for athletes.

Unofficial Advisers

Your Coach

Picture the following scene: The catalog states that course A is a requirement for graduation. Unfortunately, it conflicts with your team's practice time (a common problem). You talk with a teammate who says the word going around is that you don't really have to take that course in order to graduate. You check with your coach, who says the same thing and adds that a number of students have gotten by without it. You take the coach's advice and don't take the course.

Sometime later, you're ready to graduate. You go through the process (by filing the proper form) of getting your college record officially evaluated. Now, let's really set the scene and say that your family is coming to the graduation ceremony and you have a job waiting for you once you have the diploma in hand.

In taking the final official look at your academic record, however, the university administration finds that you haven't taken a course that is required for graduation. It happens to be the one that conflicted with the team practice schedule some time ago. You tell the school official that the coach said you didn't have to take it and that a lot of people graduated without it. The university administrator is likely to say that the advice given you was not only unofficial, but bad. You will be stuck with having to take that course before graduating. It will be frustrating and embarrassing to have to change your plans, and it will likely cost you the job.

This is just one of many potential disasters that can occur when students take hearsay for truth. Even though coaches are hired and paid by the college, their advice on academic matters is unofficial and may serve their own needs more than yours. Many coaches care very much in a personal sense about the welfare of their athletes. At the same time, however, many *primarily* care that their athletes not only stay eligible but also have time and energy free for their sport. When your academic growth and the team's welfare are not in conflict, the advice coming from the coach may be in your best interest. But if there is conflict between athletic and academic interests, you very likely may be hurt in the long run if you follow the coach's advice blindly.

Because this conflict of interest is a common problem, many schools prohibit coaches from advising athletes on academic matters. If such a rule doesn't exist at your college or university, it may be difficult to determine whether the advice the coach is giving you is in your best interest. Suffice it to say that there are better sources for advice on academic, career, and other nonsports matters than your team coach.

The Grapevine

Advice received through the student grapevine may offer some good leads, but don't make decisions based solely on this kind of information. The grapevine carries much information about good courses and bad courses. It can tell you which professors are better than others (although you shouldn't confuse easier or more entertaining with better). The grapevine can help you locate a faculty member who has good contacts in your career area. The grapevine also often carries information about summer jobs and may lead you to a source of financial aid you hadn't known about. The grapevine may even remind you of approaching deadlines and other important information that slipped your mind. It can provide you with much good and useful information, but you can't bank on it for *reliable* information about requirements, rules, and regulations. Official information should come from official advisers.

T he grapevine can give you some good information, but don't make decisions based *solely* on what you learn from it.

Special Organizations That Help Athletes

Several organizations have been formed specifically to help student-athletes achieve academic progress. These organizations are geared especially for athletes who feel trapped at a school where the coaches' interests are aimed mainly at keeping their athletes eligible for sports or where the school's support system has not been helpful.

The Athlete Career Connection was founded by Arthur Ashe and Kevin Dowdell. Its purpose is to help student-athletes complete their college degree and have a satisfying and successful career outside of sports. This goal is approached in four ways. (1) High-profile athletes who have name recognition are brought onto college and university campuses to give public talks to student-athletes about the importance of education and about the opportunities that are available to college graduates. (2) Student-athletes are provided with information about careers in professional sports, including key financial information that is not widely known. (3) Student-athletes are put in touch with companies that have special interest in the many positive qualities that athletes can bring to the workplace. (4) Once former student-athletes have graduated and are in their first job, they are connected with corporate mentors and mentors from the organization who help guide and assess career progress and provide follow-up to assist their development.

The Center for the Study of Sport in Society (CSSS) is concerned with helping further the education of athletes in junior high school through college. It is geared particularly toward helping current and former professional athletes complete their undergraduate degree. CSSS also helps prepare athletes for careers after their days in competition have ended. It is headquartered at Northeastern University in Boston, but a number of colleges and universities around the country are affiliated with it and have staff who counsel athletes about their education and postplaying career.

At PACE (Professional Athlete's Career Enterprise) Sports, the staff consists of former athletes and coaches who have experience in business and counseling. It is their job to provide assistance to athletes who want to move from the playing field into the business world. PACE has helped over 1,000 professional, college, and amateur athletes make the transition to careers beyond sports. PACE also provides guidance to athletes who want to continue or complete their schooling—especially those who have interrupted their college education. Through career workshops, PACE counselors provide help in such areas as resume preparation, interview skills, and developing strategies for career advancement.

The Women's Sports Foundation was founded by Billie Jean King, Donna DeVarona, and Carol Mann, whose respective areas of competition are tennis, swimming, and golf. Its purpose is to serve as an active advocate of equal opportunity for females in sports. The foundation supplies information on college athletic scholarships; careers in medicine, education, business, and communications (among others); drug use; eating disorders; nutrition; and Title IX to female athletes in all sports. It does not provide individual counseling. The foundation offers some financial aid through its Travel and Training Fund.

For more information about these organizations, contact:

Athlete Career Connection
4201 Cathedral Avenue, NW, Suite 102-E
Washington, DC 20016
202-966-1490

Center for the Study of Sport in Society
Northeastern University
360 Huntington Avenue
Boston, MA 02115
617-437-5815

PACE Sports, Inc.
9625 Black Mountain Road, Suite 305
San Diego, CA 92126
619-530-0700

Women's Sports Foundation
342 Madison Avenue, Suite 728
New York, NY 10173
212-972-9170

Athlete Profile

Student-Athlete Founders for Nine Years Due to Lack of Counseling

Phil Gayle grew up playing basketball in Bayonne, New Jersey. He attracted the attention of the coach at Jersey City State, who got him into college through the Educational Opportunity Program (EOP) and found some nonathletic financial aid for him. Phil's EOP counselor enrolled him in basic English and mathematics courses, but after that, according to Phil, "Counseling fell into my own hands. I really had no counseling my freshman year. I took courses here and there and did pretty well, making about a 2.9 GPA, but with no direction." But Phil wasn't happy at Jersey City State, so he dropped out.

"I thought I could do better for myself, so I went out to a junior college in California." At junior college, Phil generally took what his coach suggested, usually courses that the coach and the athletics director taught (first aid, sports officiating, etc.).

"I felt that I eventually wanted to go on to a four-year school, but nobody told me how or what to take. I wanted to go to the University of Hawaii at Hilo, but my JC coach never made the contacts he said he was going to make for me. The coach at Eastern Montana was interested [in me] and got me a partial scholarship, but I didn't know I wouldn't be eligible to play because I never graduated from my junior college. Then, somehow my old coach got me an A.A. degree. This kept me eligible but didn't do much to help me learn to work toward a goal.

"I still didn't know I needed certain classes in different areas to get a B.A. I thought I could just take what I wanted. The coaches seemed happy enough to pick my classes for me anyway."

But after attending three schools over a six-year period, Phil was still two years of course work away from graduation. When his eligibility for basketball expired, so did his scholarship, and Phil left Eastern Montana. He returned to California, where he made his living for a while pushing a mop in a hospital.

"I knew I wanted more from my life than that. I felt I could be a pretty good basketball coach but knew I couldn't get a job coaching a school team without a degree. I was never dumb; I just didn't have good direction, either from myself or from those who were supposedly taking care of me."

Nine years after graduating from high school, Phil Gayle was finally close to earning a bachelor's degree in education. What would he have done differently? *"From day one, I would seek counseling. I would play basketball again, but I would also keep an eye on my future. I would stress academics more and take courses that would help me progress — not just stay eligible for sports. And I would find someone to advise me correctly about what I need to do to earn my degree."*

4

Drugs and Sports

*Recreational Drugs . . . Hard Drugs . . .
Performance-Enhancing Drugs . . . Drug
Testing . . . Strategies for Competing
Without Drugs*

You are hurt. You are in a slump, depressed, or stressed out. The person you have to beat is bigger or better than you. Your teammates are taking drugs, and you don't want to seem different. You feel like celebrating a victory with something extra.

"Just say no" is not an answer or a solution to the drug problem, either within sports or in society in general. Telling drug users or those thinking about becoming users to "just say no" doesn't work because it fails to address the reasons that lead people into taking drugs. People who use drugs believe that they need these drugs to help them through rough times, to make them feel better, or to help improve their performance in some activity of importance to them. Just saying no might work if the drugs didn't work—but they often do work. Unfortunately, they hurt more than help, which is why there are laws and rules against taking many of the drugs discussed in this chapter and why we are against your taking them. We will present you with the facts about what drugs do *for* you and what they do *to* you. We hope that through knowing the facts you also will conclude that you'll be better off *not* using them.

Jonathan Lehrman, M.D., consulted on this chapter. Dr. Lehrman is coauthor, with Lawrence L. Ruff and E. T. Mellor, of *A Practical Guide for Handling Drug Crises* (Springfield, Ill.: C. C. Thomas, 1980).

Drugs present several specific problems for athletes. Many people think of athletes as having high status and want to get close to them. If you are an athlete, everybody seems to want to know you, or at least know about you. One way people try to get close to athletes is by giving or buying them things. A booster may give an athlete a few dollars "to help out." Someone might treat an athlete to a hamburger or a drink. Someone else may provide something to help the athlete compete — a pill or some white powder. It's cool to know athletes, and it's cool to do something you aren't supposed to do, such as driving a car before you get your license, drinking underage, or taking drugs. You may never have thought of taking illegal drugs before, but now someone may offer them to you — even for free (at first).

I liked being on the edge. Most athletes do. We're thrill seekers. Athletics itself is a high. . . . Taking steroids was just another way of living on the edge.

Tommie Chaikin, former University of
South Carolina football player [1]

It's strange to see athletes who work and train so hard to succeed in their sport and avoid injury voluntarily inflict injury on themselves just because someone offered a short-term, meaningless thrill in the form of drugs. Drugs are dangerous and illegal for everybody, but for athletes they directly and immediately threaten what motivates them the most — the right and the opportunity to compete in sports.

Drugs such as alcohol, marijuana, cocaine, crack cocaine, crank, and heroin and other hard drugs are used to get high or to forget about problems. Steroids, human growth hormone, beta-blockers, and some of the recreational drugs are taken by some athletes in the belief that they will improve performance. We will discuss those that you are likely to encounter beginning with recreational drugs — including some that you probably never considered to be drugs — followed by hard drugs and performance-enhancing drugs.

Recreational Drugs

Recreational drugs are those taken initially for pleasure, escape, or relief of stress. The user can become addicted, which means that he or she takes them from habit or physical need rather than for "recreation."

Caffeine

We tend not to think of caffeine as a drug, but it is a drug because it affects our bodies and alters our behavior. Approximately 200 milligrams of caffeine — the amount found in two cups of coffee, four or five cola drinks, and one or two diet or stimulant pills such as Dexatrim or Nodoz — acts as a fairly mild stimulant. When a person ingests as much as 500 milligrams of caffeine (four or five cups of coffee or a combination of the above substances) within a few hours, heart rate and respiration both climb markedly. A very large intake of caffeine can result in a heart attack, and, if a pregnant woman drinks a great amount of coffee, tea, or cola or takes caffeine pills, her baby could suffer from birth defects.

While drinking a cup of coffee a day isn't bad, people can develop a dependency on caffeine — the feeling that they need it to get through the day. When a caffeine-dependent person abruptly tries to stop using it, that person may develop headaches and be easily irritated, which often leads him or her to begin using caffeine again.

Tobacco

Cigarettes have long been referred to as coffin nails. Whether it is smoked, chewed, or wedged between cheek and gum, tobacco is a killer. Nicotine is the addictive part of tobacco, while the tars cause cancer. People often start using tobacco to be cool, to appear grown-up, or to help them cope with stress; ultimately they use it because they get hooked on it. Tobacco — smokable or smokeless — is a major health risk that leads to cancer, lung disease, and heart attacks. Using it is one of the hardest habits to kick.

While smoked tobacco leads to lung cancer, smokeless tobacco (snuff and chew) causes cancers of the mouth and digestive tract. A pack of cigarettes or more a day is *the* most significant risk factor for developing heart attacks — an even greater threat than high levels of cholesterol.

Alcohol

Alcohol is a commonly used and commonly abused legal drug, and many who use it don't realize the harm it can cause. Alcohol is generally accepted socially when used in moderation. When used to excess, it can result in poor judgment and impaired physical coordination. (Ironically though, alcohol can make you feel *more* coordinated.) It can bring on a range of moods, from relaxation to loss of self-control, which can lead to anger and violence.

Drinking combined with driving is the single greatest threat to the lives of college-age males. Pregnant women who consume alcohol can seriously damage their unborn children. Long-term damage from alcohol abuse includes cirrhosis of the liver and brain deterioration. Moderate drinking carries few of these harmful effects, although keeping alcohol consumption moderate can be very difficult. Withdrawal from alcohol abuse is extremely difficult.

Amphetamines

Amphetamines are habit-forming stimulants, ingested in pill form or snorted, and known variously as speed, crank, uppers, and bennies. A smokable amphetamine known as ice has also made an appearance and is extremely dangerous. Amphetamines stimulate the brain and make the user feel more energetic, alert, and primed for action. They also mask pain, reduce or delay fatigue, and increase confidence and aggressiveness. Their ability to mask pain can present a serious problem for the athletes who use them. Not feeling the pain of an injury can cause an athlete to push a minor injury into something serious or permanent.

Not feeling the pain of an injury can cause an athlete to push a minor injury into something serious or permanent.

Although a feeling of confidence is something we all seek, relying on amphetamines to achieve it will ultimately lead to poor decision making and poor performance. Amphetamines interfere with the user's perception of what is actually happening, and they can cloud an athlete's sense of timing, recall of plays and formations, and ability to strategize.

Real time and drug time are different. Some amphetamines will make you believe that your reactions are lightning quick when in fact you are moving more slowly than normal. Others may cause you to react faster than you practiced, which could lead to penalties and poor coordination with teammates. It's better to trust your own trained body and mind, your coaches, and your teammates for emotional drive and timing than to rely on drugs such as speed. Amphetamines won't add anything to that formula — they are more likely to detract from it.

Cocaine, Crack, Marijuana, and Hallucinogens

Cocaine, crack, marijuana, and hallucinogens such as LSD, peyote, PCP, and psilocybin mushrooms have come to be known as recreational drugs because people use them to achieve pleasurable feelings, to socialize, and to temporarily escape from problems. However, playing around with these drugs is like playing catch in the fast lane of a highway at rush hour.

Crack, manufactured purified cocaine, is the drug's most dangerous form. Crack use has spread in recent years because it is much cheaper than powdered cocaine, and, since it is smoked, the effect is more immediate and intense. Crack is among the most highly addictive of all drugs and has been known to addict first-time users.

The lady [cocaine] is a monster, a home wrecker and a life wrecker. In the body of a skilled athlete, she's a destroyer of talent. Right this minute she's spoiling the careers of great athletes you pay to watch.

Don Reese, former football player with
the Miami Dolphins, New Orleans Saints,
and San Diego Chargers [2]

From the NFL's All Pro Lawrence Taylor to the late Len Bias, the University of Maryland's All-America basketball star who died of a cocaine overdose in 1986, athletes who use recreational drugs are hot news. Ken Anderson, former All Pro quarterback of the Cincinnati Bengals, says, "All athletes now are really under a microscope. If your neighbor gets picked up for possession of drugs, it's buried in the papers. If it's a player, it's headlines."[3] But more important than the issue of whether or not the public should know about an athlete's private behavior is the reality of the effect that cocaine and other recreational drugs can have on a college athlete's academic performance, athletics career, and life.

The Real Cost of Recreational Drugs

How are these drugs likely to affect your schoolwork? Some students believe that cocaine and marijuana increase their stamina for studying and loosen them up for tests. While recreational drugs can make you feel better, remember that's only temporary. The reality is that you are likely to feel better while doing worse because the drugs impair your judgment.

The effects are even greater in sports. Increased stamina and a relaxed attitude can help performance in some sports. But while cocaine (for example) may make you feel good, it actually decreases muscle power, reflex time, and visual coordination. Altered judgment and a faulty sense of timing can harm an athlete and his or her teammates. Detection of drug use can jeopardize an athlete's career.

What about the dollar cost of drugs and what users sometimes do to get the money? What about the legal fees involved in getting caught and the emotional cost to the drug user's family? All of these factors should be considered and weighed if you're thinking about using drugs. The decision to take drugs is a decision that *you* make—not your parents, coach, friends, or anyone else. Others may lead you to the door, but *you* walk through it.

Recreational drugs may give a thrill, but they can lead to a ruined career, jail time, and death. At the very least, sooner or later taking them will change your life in a way you won't want. It may be difficult to stop using drugs if you've already started, and you may need help to stop, but it *can* be done.

Hard Drugs

Narcotics

Narcotics and barbiturates present a group of drugs that are neither recreational nor performance enhancing in any direct way. A narcotic, such as heroin, is a drug that dulls the senses and relieves pain and is used to escape from reality. It also causes severe depression. Narcotics are physically addictive. Becoming free of them may require a very difficult withdrawal period in a controlled hospital setting.

Codeine and synthetic narcotics are often prescribed in pill form for pain relief and to treat injuries. When they are over-used — that is, abused — they are addictive.

You may have heard that if you stay away from hard drugs, such as heroin, you won't get hooked. Or you may believe that you are different and can stop using anytime you want. The fact is, you can become addicted to drugs other than heroin, and, whatever the narcotic, it is difficult to remain a small user, because, as your body adapts to the poison, you need heavier doses each time you use it to get as high as you did the time before.

Barbiturates and Other Tranquilizers

Barbiturates and other tranquilizers reduce tension and anxiety by depressing the central nervous system. They allow the user to escape pressure and anxiety, to relax, and to ease emotional pain — for a time. They also alter the user's sense of time and place, cause loss of judgment and self-control, slow reflexes, and cause sedation. Some people will use tranquilizers, such as Quaaludes, to alter the effects of other drugs. Mixing these drugs, however, can result in an overdose and lead to death.

Barbiturates and other tranquilizers are dangerous because they can lead to physical addiction and psychological dependence, although these problems are greater with barbiturates. Addiction to barbiturates can occur in as little as one month of regular use. As small an amount as 1,000 milligrams taken at one time by a new user can be deadly. Once a person has become addicted to barbiturates, withdrawal is extremely difficult and dangerous, more so than from any drug except alcohol.

As stated earlier, for those who develop the habit of using drugs, the answer to the problem is not as simple as "just say no." The problem is more complicated than deciding whether you should or shouldn't use drugs. Many drug takers have no real direction and little hope in life. How they feel right now is all they care about — drugs help them get through each day. Athletes have hope and direction. They've aimed themselves toward particular goals: their team's success and their own success. The act of striving provides its own high. Adding drugs to the mix will inevitably result in a crash. It's like putting the wrong fuel in a high-performance car. The best you can hope for is a burst of speed before the engine sputters and dies or blows up.

Performance-Enhancing Drugs

Pressure to perform comes from within athletes and from people close to them, and it can be as intense in a sport without spectators as it is in a contest in front of 50,000 fans. In an attempt to meet those expectations, some athletes resort to what are known as performance-enhancing drugs. While amphetamines (uppers), barbiturates and tranquilizers (downers), and neuromuscular enhancers are included in this category, our discussion will focus on beta-blockers, steroids, and human growth hormone.

Athletes who use drugs may view them as a necessary evil that helps them compete. They may think that taking them, especially drugs that can be obtained by prescription and are taken more or less regularly by adults outside of sports, isn't that terrible.

I always thought, if they tell me I should take it, they must think I need it. They must think I'm not good enough without it. . . . You're already nervous as hell, and somebody's telling you, "Here, you need this". . . . You can end up doing things you don't want to do.

Cindy Olavarri, competitive bicyclist [4]

Athletes begin taking performance-enhancing drugs for one reason: *fear*. They fear that they are not good enough to succeed on their own or that they'll be beaten by competitors who have gained an advantage through drugs. Cindy Olavarri, a top U.S. bicyclist, says that in bicycle racing, coaches routinely urged their athletes to take performance-enhancing drugs such as adenosinetriphosphate (ATP), along with large doses of vitamins and caffeine. A neuromuscular enhancer, ATP acts as a catalyst for muscle contraction, thus helping the muscles to respond more efficiently. It is legal in international cycling.

Olavarri's story is not simply one of following her coach's suggestions or demands (a suggestion from a coach can look very much like a demand). She made the 1984 U.S. Olympic cycling team but got kicked off for taking steroids. "That was the end of the dream that I'd had since the fourth grade," Cindy said. Worse, five years later she was suffering from a damaged liver, deteriorated ligaments and tendons, allergic reactions to foods, and a breakdown of her immune system, all of which she believes were the result of using steroids—drugs she felt she needed to remain competitive.

Beta-Blockers

Beta-blockers are a relatively new drug. They reduce anxiety and calm the jitters or butterflies. Olympic biathletes were among the first athletes to use beta-blockers. They found that they calmed the heart and that way helped to improve the marksmanship required in their sport, which combines rifle sharpshooting with cross-country skiing. In low doses, beta-blockers are effective. But for athletes, the cure is worse than the problem. The use of beta-blockers leads to confusion, memory loss, and fatigue and prevents the athlete's heart rate from reaching the optimal exercise level.

Under a new law in Canada, beta-blockers are illegal to use in any sport. The Interuniversity Athletics Union (the Canadian version of the NCAA) requires annual drug testing of athletes and will ban from competition for a full year any athlete who is found using beta-blockers. The NCAA will probably not be far behind.

Steroids

There are two distinct types of steroids. Corticosteroids are prescribed and administered by physicians to reduce inflammation and aid healing. Anabolic steroids are muscle-building chemicals and are used by some athletes. Corticosteroids are medically justifiable and are administered in limited and well-controlled doses. In contrast, anabolic steroids have little medicinal value and tend to be taken by the athletes who use them in massive, uncontrolled amounts. Some doctors will prescribe and administer moderate levels of anabolic steroids to athletes in the belief that prescribing is better than athletes' taking probably impure steroids on their own.

> *If a physician can monitor [steroids] with blood tests*
> *and so forth, it makes it safer. It doesn't make it safe,*
> *but it makes it safer.*
>
> Robert Kerr, M.D. [5]

Nonmedical personnel who sell or give anabolic steroids to athletes provide all sorts of pseudomedical advice on how to use the drugs and offer various assurances about how safe they are. If you believe them, you might as well take flying lessons from a flight attendant.

Athletes have been taking anabolic steroids to improve performance for three decades. Such use began in the 1960s in the USSR, East Germany, and other Soviet Bloc countries, whose athletes started to dominate international events around the same time. Subsequently, American, Canadian, and Western European athletes who competed in those events adopted the use of steroids to gain equal competitive stature. For years, scientists said that there was no proof about the athletic-performance benefits of steroid use. But athletes and coaches, seeing some athletes gain size, strength, and stamina much more quickly than could be expected from ordinary training, knew better.

Anabolic steroids can make an athlete larger by increasing protein synthesis in the body, which helps to produce more muscle mass. The athlete needs to train vigorously and take protein supplements in order for this to happen. From the 1960s through the 1980s, some athletes found that taking more than the prescribed dose could lead to even more muscle growth and weight gain over an even shorter period of time. The increased dose provided a shortcut in which the effects of several years of training could be packed into a few months. Athletes began to stack their steroids — taking several different kinds at the same time or alternately in order to reap the special benefits of each kind. Another method for using steroids is cycling — taking different steroids in turn over three- to twelve-week periods. Stacking and cycling are based on the belief that more is better.

As mentioned earlier, some researchers have said that there is no direct evidence of the muscle-and-mass benefits of steroids. But no matter what the scientists say, athletes know that they get bigger, stronger, faster, and more aggressive and that they have greater stamina and desire to work out as a result of using steroids. The bottom line, or so athletes who take steroids believe, is to do better in competition.

But *is* competing better really the bottom line? From an ethical point of view, steroids destroy the essence of sports competition. When steroids or other drugs help determine who wins or loses, the competition is no longer about being the best athlete; instead, it becomes a competition between the best chemists. The athletes merely serve as performing machines — tossed aside and replaced when they break down.

Effects of Steroids Use [6]

Men	Women
Increased muscle mass (with protein supplement)	Increased muscle mass (with protein supplement)
Heightened work drive	Heightened work drive
Increased lean body mass	Increased lean body mass
Growth of breasts	Shrinkage of breasts
Impotency	Growth of facial hair (irreversible)
Violent behavior	Growth of body hair (irreversible)
Shrinkage of testes	Growth of clitoris (irreversible)
Acne	Acne
Hastens balding	Causes balding
Clogged arteries	Clogged arteries
Aggressiveness	Aggressiveness
Depression	Depression
Liver damage	Liver damage

Maybe the ethics of competition are not as important to you as being successful, especially if you believe ethics will cost you a career in sports. In a society that rewards success much more than honesty, you can't really be faulted for focusing on the short-term bottom line. But ethics aside, the reality is that steroids can destroy the people who use them. That is why fifteen states (as of this writing), the International Olympic Committee, the NCAA, and the NFL have all made the use of steroids by athletes illegal. The preceding table shows what steroids do for athletes and what they do to them.

The links between steroid abuse and some of these side effects are clear. The level of naturally occurring steroids (testosterone) in a person's system is regulated by the hypothalamus and pituitary glands of the brain. When steroids are taken, the body's natural response is to shut down its own production of testosterone. Several of the side effects of steroids listed in the chart occur because of the chemical balancing act conducted by the brain (called a "negative feedback loop" in medicine). A shutdown of the body's production of testosterone can also explain how young people can actually stunt their growth by taking steroids.

No question . . . there have been deaths from steroids —
attributed to them, cancer of the liver, cancer of the
kidney.

Irving Dardik, M.D., chairman of the USOC
Sports Medicine Committee [7]

Organs such as the liver and kidney are directly affected by the use of steroids, although symptoms may not immediately accompany damage to them. This is because organs make adjustments and continue to function at partial capacity while they are being damaged. Only when they have been stressed and damaged beyond a critical point do symptoms begin to appear. By then, the organ may be beyond recovery or repair. In short, don't look for a sign from your organs to tell you when to stop taking drugs. By the time you see or feel the symptoms, it could be too late.

Human Growth Hormone

Human growth hormone (HGH) is harvested from the pituitary glands of dead humans.[8] While steroids can help to develop more massive muscles and added weight, HGH develops greater height and longer limbs — *but only when the body's natural growth system allows it.*

People gain height primarily at the epiphyseal plates, the sections near each end of the long bones of the legs and arms where new cells are produced. In the growth process, the body adds cells that lengthen these bones at these specific points. The body then adds muscle, ligament, tendon, and other tissues to match the growing bones. At some time during adolescence or early adulthood, the epiphyseal plates harden and allow no additional cells to add to bone length. This is when a person's adult height and maximum limb length have been reached. No amount of exercise, stretching, or drugs will increase them.

If a person who has reached adult growth takes HGH, the bones will grow thicker, not longer, resulting in a caveman look (in medical terminology the condition is known as acromegaly). There will be some muscle growth, primarily to support the increased thickness and weight of the bones, but much of the bone thickening occurs in the face, hands, and feet, adding little to athletic performance. Harmful side effects include enlarged heart and kidney, congestive heart failure, diabetes, hypertension, and, in men, shrinkage of the testes.

Assessing the Risks

Some athletes are willing to risk physical and psychological damage for the competitive edge performance-enhancing drugs might provide. Here are a few athletes who took that risk.

- Steven Courson, a football player for the Tampa Bay Buccaneers, tells of stacking several kinds of steroids, including Dianabol, Androl-50, Anavar, and Winstrol. While still in his early 30s, Courson faced a heart transplant because his own heart had lost its elasticity.

- Jim Goulah, a bodybuilder who admitted to using steroids in order to become competitive, suffered a massive stroke at the age of 34. He has had to relearn how to speak, read, use his left hand, and recognize his family.

- Tommie Chaikin, a former University of South Carolina football player, took HGH along with steroids. Telling his own story in the October 24, 1988, issue of *Sports Illustrated*, Chaikin described his bouts with anxiety, paranoia, rage, and violence. At the age of 23, Chaikin found himself sitting in his dormitory room with a loaded .357 Magnum pressed under his chin, one slight twitch from ending his life.

- The *New England Journal of Medicine* reported a case in which an athlete became addicted to steroids.[9]

I was in bad shape, very bad shape. From the steroids. It had all come down from the steroids, the crap I'd taken to get big and strong and aggressive so I could play this game that I love.

Tommie Chaikin [10]

You might think that you can get away with taking small doses of steroids and still gain the strength and size that you desire, but steroids don't work that way. The doses must continually be increased to build more muscle because, as noted, the human body compensates for injected and ingested steroids by producing less of its own natural testosterone. (This helps to explain the effects on testes, breasts, and sexual potency.)

The anxiety that leads some athletes to believe that they need steroids in order to be competitive can also lead them to believe that their opponents might be megadosing and so drive them to use even larger amounts of steroids. As stated earlier, fear generates the idea to take steroids in the first place and is the reason that some athletes resort to using clearly unhealthful levels. Put yourself in that situation. You don't *want* to take the drugs. You don't *want* to damage yourself. You want a clean sport. But if your opponent is gaining an advantage by using drugs, what else can you do? Haven't you always been told to do whatever it takes to succeed in sports? Until regulations and enforcement compel those you compete against to stop taking steroids, the cost to you if you don't take them could be great and include losing contests and your place on the team (the latter may mean losing your financial aid package). It's a serious problem, which is why drug testing of college athletes has begun. The choice you have to make about whether or not to use drugs can be extremely difficult. If good health and believing in what is right remain most important to you, you'll refuse to take the drugs.

> *Drug abuse . . . has become a way of life for many ath-*
> *letes and a constant preoccupation even for those who*
> *abstain.*
>
> John Hoberman, professor of languages,
> University of Texas at Austin [11]

Drug Testing

Drug abuse is a problem for society in general and sports in particular. People disagree, however, about whether testing for drug use is the answer to the problem. *Random* drug testing of athletes — testing without warning and at any time of the year — has been approved by the NCAA as a means of circumventing those who try to beat the tests, but some college athletes and professional athlete unions have resisted random testing, claiming that it represents a violation of constitutional rights to privacy.[12]

In several cases, college athletes have sued their school or the NCAA for making drug testing mandatory for the privilege of competing on a team. According to one study, however, nearly two thirds of college athletes favor random drug testing, essentially giving up their right to privacy in order to ensure that their sports are rid of performance-enhancing drugs.[13]

Throughout the year, the NCAA randomly tests Division I-A and I-AA football and basketball players for steroid use and for the drugs that may be used to block steroid detection. The presence of either type of drug in an athlete's system is considered evidence of guilt. At championship events in all NCAA divisions for all sports, testing is done for steroids and other drugs, including recreational drugs such as cocaine and marijuana. Wider testing has been recommended by Richard Schultz, NCAA executive director.

It's clear, however, that some athletes will still try to use drugs to gain an advantage, and in the absence of random testing it will be easier for them to do so. Fear that they will be at a competitive disadvantage will lead even more athletes to take steroids and other performance-enhancing drugs.

The presence of testing, either random or scheduled, can help you to stay away from drugs. For instance, if you don't want to use drugs, whether recreational, hard, or performance enhancing, but feel pressured by teammates or friends, you're on solid ground by refusing, because you could get caught by a drug test.

Scientists persist in devising more and more accurate tests, while drug makers and takers continue to find more devious ways to avoid detection.[14] But periodically, the testers close the gap on the users, and a handful of athletes are found to be using drugs. They are then banned from competition or stripped of their awards and records, as were gold-medal-winning sprinter Ben Johnson and several other athletes at the 1988 Olympics.

It seems that steroid users and the testers have their own competition going on. The users look for more sophisticated drugs that can either avoid detection or be eliminated from the body before tests can measure them. Steroids taken orally can be ingested up to two weeks before a test without detection, although this varies with the individual. Such factors as rate of metabolism and diet, body fat composition, amount of drug, how long drugs were taken, and type of drug also affect detectability. Because body fat retains steroids, some injected steroids can be detected several months after the last dose. Exertion and stress of competition can release steroids stored in body fat and cause them to register on tests even though the athlete may have stopped using them long before.

Dr. James Puffer, chair of the NCAA Committee on Competitive Safeguards and Medical Aspects of Sports, believes that many more athletes use banned drugs than are caught by the tests. They attempt to avoid detection by "cycling off" the drugs in time, by using methods to block detection, or by avoiding sports events at which they know testing will take place. When drug tests were administered unannounced at the 1983 Pan American games, only nineteen athletes were convicted of illegal drug use, but eleven others pulled out of the competition before being tested.

Meg Ritchie, strength and conditioning coach at the University of Arizona, suggests that the use of steroids be legalized because they are "simply an avenue to success along with new training methods, sports psychology, food supplements, etc."[15] But that position ignores the reasons that steroids are increasingly being banned: first, the harm they do to those who take them and, second, the harm they do to competitive sports by forcing more athletes to take them in order to remain competitive.

The weight of law and public opinion is turning against the use of steroids by athletes.

Ritchie suggests that having laws against steroids could be turning people into criminals, which is like saying that laws against theft turn citizens into criminals. The trend, however, as evidence about their dangers builds, is toward criminalizing the use of steroids. As the 1990s began, more than fifty bills in state legislatures across the country addressed steroid use by athletes. The weight of law and public opinion is turning against the use of steroids by athletes. Even in Soviet Bloc countries, where steroid use by athletes began, performance-enhancing drugs are falling out of favor. While some athletes may still want to take the steroid shortcut to success, public and legal pressure are likely to turn that tide.

An ingenious solution to the problem is the suggestion to divide sports competition into the naturals, who would be certified as free of steroids and other artificial aids, and the freaks, who would be allowed to ingest and inject whatever they want without limits or laws. The groups would compete separately. Given a clear choice, the public might prefer to see natural athletes compete, with the "freak show" suffering an unnatural death or being devalued to the level of professional wrestling.

Until the time comes when competitors stop using performance-enhancing drugs, the choice is yours.

- Compete with the artificial assistance of drugs; worry about getting caught; jeopardize your reputation, your eligibility, and, possibly, your college education; and do significant damage to your body and your mind.

OR

- Compete healthily, legally, drug free, and with self-respect.

We can't claim that drugs such as steroids have no effect on the size and strength of athletes. But athletes shouldn't believe that taking drugs is the only way to match the size and strength of their opponents. The cost of the second choice is more time, effort, and self-discipline to match the strength and size of drug users. The cost of the first choice is injury, illness, and, perhaps, death.

Let's get back . . . to those days, well within my memory, when every athlete thought that the only things he or she needed megadoses of were discipline, grace, and courage.

Edwin Moses, world champion hurdler [16]

Strategies for Competing Without Drugs

Taking drugs isn't the only way to increase your size and strength. There are safer, more natural ways that do less damage to you and to your sport. In his book *Dying to Win,* Dr. Michael Asken suggests several drug-free tactics for success, including:

1. **Eating better.** Protein should be a major part of your diet, as many athletes in weight training know, but the rest of your diet needs to be balanced to help metabolize the protein and provide the energy needed for hard work. It's foolish and futile to try to build muscle tissue efficiently on a diet of protein powder and greasy fast food.

2. **Training better and more often through commitment and self-discipline.** You'll have to put in more hours, but if you train scientifically and efficiently, the time commitment can remain reasonable. Few coaches know as much about physical training as exercise specialists, while the physical specimens developed at many health clubs may look good without having a body that is athletically trained. Find an exercise specialist with a strong background in the physical sciences who can provide you with an efficient program. Your college's physical education department is likely to have such a person.

3. **Positive mental imaging.** Seeing yourself as a success *before* you try something can help you come closer to your goal, especially if you tend to doubt yourself or imagine failure. You know how energized you get when victory is close. You can give yourself this natural energy by visualizing success before you set out on a task. Imagine the pleasure of each day's success before you begin a workout, then go for it. Better yet, imagine the *next* day's success at the end of your current day's workout. A corner of your mind will be laying the groundwork and energizing you for the following day.

4. **Setting directed goals.** This means planning each step along the way to success. A technique to help you accomplish this is Visuo-Motor Behavior Rehearsal, or VMBR. VMBR means combining positive mental imagery — seeing success in your mind's eye — with small, well-planned steps down the road to success. If your ultimate success entails getting from point A to point Z, then your first goal is to get to point B. Taking drugs to find success is an attempt to leap over the middle steps, but drugs leave you vulnerable to a crash landing. Taking the drug shortcut may mean missing your major goal entirely and doing permanent damage to yourself. Don't be seduced by the images of the few athletes who made it by (or despite) using drugs. We seldom hear about the many who crashed short of success because of the drugs.[17]

Despite awareness of the dangers of taking drugs, the temptation to take them remains. When a particular kind of drug may help you to compete, you may ask, "Why not?" To answer that question, consider how taking it will affect the things that are important to you. A list of those things will probably include:

- Family
- Education/schoolwork
- Personal ethics/religion/God
- Health (current)
- Health (future)
- Sports career
- Other career
- Friends/people liking you

55

- Recognition/fame
- Physical attractiveness
- Money
- Security
- Happiness
- Accomplishments in sports

If you are using a drug (or drugs) or are considering using one (or more than one), write its name or the category that it's in at the top of a blank piece of paper. You'll know which of the bulleted items are important to you, so list them in your own order of importance, and, of course, add any other things important to you that are missing. Mark a plus (+) next to the items that would be enhanced by using that particular drug, a minus (–) next to those that would be diminished, and a zero next to items that would not be affected. This exercise will help you see more clearly what particular drugs do for you and what they do to you.

People don't always make wise decisions. Too often they take the path that may seem obvious or that they are pushed toward. Only when they are down that path and paying the price do they regret it. Knowledge about drugs, the self-assessment techniques offered here, and hard thinking can help to save your health and your athletics career.

5

Special Considerations for Black Athletes

*Your Choice: Exploitation or Fair Exchange . . .
The Differences Between Black and White
Athletes and What They Mean . . . Proposition
48 . . . Graduate Instead of Just Spending Time
in College . . . Communication . . . Getting Help
from Others . . . Hang out with Friends Who
Are on the Success Track . . . Stereotypes . . . The
Cold, Hard Realities of a Career in Professional
Sports for Black Athletes . . . Career Goals*

Well over 90 percent of collegiate athletes who are members of a minority group are black, and this chapter was written in order to address the problems they face. The three main problems that tend to affect black student-athletes are as follows.

- **Black athletes focus too much on a professional sports career.** Too many black athletes believe they'll make it in pro sports. Very few will actually get paid to play, and only a fraction of those will spend enough time in the pros to call it a career. An unrealistic focus on a professional career can result in neglected studies, failure to graduate, and missed opportunities to develop other career interests.
- **Black athletes are misled and exploited by others.** People who run college athletics programs care mainly about winning and not enough about the well-being and growth of their athletes. Coaches, college officials, and alumni often

want student-athletes only for their talent and may not care whether the athlete gets a degree or much else in return. This can happen to any athlete, but it seems to happen more to black athletes.

- **Black athletes exploit themselves.** Black athletes often fail to acquire the learning skills and attitudes needed for success in a career and in life outside of sports. This occurs when the athlete studies less, takes easy classes instead of important and challenging ones, and does not choose a major carefully. Study with a purpose (the way you practice your sport), take courses that are tough but rewarding, and choose a major that supports your career goals. If you fail to do any of these, you are exploiting yourself.

Harry Edwards has for twenty years been the strongest and most eloquent voice for minority athletes in general and black athletes in particular.

> It is Black athletes themselves who must shoulder a substantial portion of the responsibility for improving Black circumstances and outcomes in American sports. Black athletes must insist upon intellectual discipline no less than athletic discipline among themselves, and upon educational integrity in athletic programs rather than, as is all too often the case, merely seeking the easiest route to maintaining athletic eligibility. If Black athletes fail to take a conscious, active, and informed role in changing the course and character of Black sports involvement, nothing done by any other party to this tragic situation is likely to be effective or lasting—if for no other reason than the fact that a slave cannot be freed against his will.[1]

Your Choice: Exploitation or Fair Exchange

College athletes give time, effort, and a winning attitude—in addition to their talent—to the school and the coach. In return, the school and the coach give athletes the opportunity to be on the team and, in some instances, a scholarship or a job to help pay for school. But the most important and lasting thing that any student-athlete gets in college is an education that leads to a career. If the school or the coach gets in the way of that education, the student-athlete is being exploited and is not getting fair exchange for the time, effort, sweat, and pain put into the sport.

Student-athletes who shortchange their education—by taking easy courses, by cheating on tests or assignments, and by not growing with the experience of college—are exploiting themselves. Research comparing black and white students shows that blacks were not as well prepared for college and were less confident about their ability to do college-level work.[2] The research also showed that black athletes took easier courses and majors, they took fewer courses each term, and they cheated more. If a student-athlete who is a member of a minority group is not well prepared for college, it may be the fault of people who exploited that student-athlete in high school, when the athlete was younger and didn't know better. In college, student-athletes who cheat and take the easy road are exploiting themselves. A college degree, particularly a degree in a field that interests you, is the best way to avoid or overcome exploitation.

Black athletes must insist upon intellectual discipline no less than athletic discipline.

In college, what you do one year allows you to do better the next year and every year until you graduate. Sports can pay for college, and competing can be fun. But you must force yourself to look past the good times and begin immediately (Today! Right now!) to prepare for life in a way that will not allow you to be exploited, where you have the weapons—skills, knowledge, and awareness—to fight exploitation. A good education gives you those weapons and the power to fight for yourself and your family. The business of a college is to prepare its students for the future. You need to make sure now, as far as your own future is concerned, that that business is being done.

What if you feel you are already behind in your schoolwork? What you do now will show what you are made of. Every tick of the clock or stride closer to the finish line gives you less time to close the gap, so you've got to make your move now.

The Differences Between Black and White Athletes and What They Mean

A recent study of college athletics revealed some interesting comparisons between black and white football and basketball players from NCAA Division I schools.[3]

College Entrance

Black student-athletes tend to have lower high school grade point averages and tend to score lower than whites on college entrance exams (SAT and ACT). Some people see this as a racial difference, but the scores relate more to family income than to race. In other words, blacks who come from homes with a high income score better than whites who come from low-income households. Since you are already in college and have the opportunity to earn your degree and make a good living, things can be better for your children than they were for you. It is likely that your children will go to better schools than you did and be much better prepared for college than you were. By getting a college degree, you can turn things around for yourself and your family.

Time Spent in Sports Compared with Schoolwork

Black athletes tend to spend more time in their sport than they do studying or going to class. Black athletes also take fewer classes each term than whites and miss more class sessions. So it should not be surprising that black athletes tend to get lower grades than white athletes, and they tend to be on academic probation more often. On the other hand, black athletes tend to believe they are capable of earning better grades than they did in high school or are currently getting in college. To get those better grades, you need to translate your confidence into action. Doing better in college requires focus on a goal and willpower — two abilities that you have already developed through sports. You need to apply that goal orientation and willpower to schoolwork. You have to *want* to succeed in college, whether you like schoolwork or not. That is the first giant step you can take toward success and graduation. You may not like lifting weights or running sprints, but you do them to succeed as an athlete. The same holds for studying — you need to do it to succeed as a student, graduate, and launch a successful career.

Career and Life Goals

Research at NCAA Division I schools shows that black college athletes more than white college athletes tend to expect a career in professional football or basketball (44 percent of blacks and 20 percent of whites).[4] That may be understandable (although unrealistic) for first-team players, but many blacks who are second- and third-team players in college still expect to become pro athletes. Only about 1 percent of college football players will ever play in the NFL. The number is about the same for the NBA and even lower in professional baseball. The high number of black athletes who expect a professional playing career reveals both exploitation and *self*-exploitation. Coaches and counselors are not telling black athletes how unrealistic their sports-career goals are, and, worse still, some black athletes are fooling themselves.

Unlike white children, who see many different potential role models in the media, black children tend to model themselves after . . . the black athlete.

Harry Edwards[5]

The good news from this research is that black athletes tend to have high life goals—happiness, health, and career and financial success—higher than those of the white athletes polled. You know that you can always improve in sports. No matter what your current level of academic ability, you can also improve it. In fact, that's what college is all about. The formula is simple. First, you convince yourself you can do it. Then, you put in the time and effort to accomplish it—and don't let anyone convince you that you can't.

Proposition 48

What if your high school didn't prepare you well enough for college, or you just didn't work hard enough in high school to prepare for college-level work? Suppose you are good enough as an athlete that the college wants you despite your grades, but you were accepted only through the NCAA's Proposition 48 or as a "special admit." Proposition 48 says that you may have to give up being an athlete during your freshman year and show that you can do college-level work.[6]

You may think this isn't fair because playing your sport is the reason—maybe the *only* reason—you want to be in college. But analyzing and accepting the situation could help you turn your life around. You know the coach thinks enough of you to keep you around for a year without using your ability to help the team. As much as you want to compete, Proposition 48 gives you a year to straighten out your schoolwork and to catch up to other students without the added time demands and pressure involved in sports.[7]

I have to be positive about this [Proposition 48]. It could be the best thing that could happen to me in the long run. There are a lot of great players back home on the streets after [their] eligibility ran out with no job and no degree.

Tharon Mayes, basketball player,
Florida State University [8]

You can build up your learning skills during a year without sports much more easily than if you were playing—but not if you waste time or feel sorry for yourself because you aren't competing. If you listen to your counselors and attack your schoolwork, you can prove to yourself and others that you are able to do college-level work. (You'll learn how to do these things in subsequent chapters in this book.)

Graduate Instead of Just Spending Time in College

Blacks who graduate from college earn 40 to 50 percent more in their lifetime than those who graduate from high school only. No matter what ethnic or racial group they belong to, college graduates earn a lot more money and have higher status as well. Many thousands of jobs across the entire spectrum of the work world are open only to people with a college degree.

You should be proud of getting into college and being a college athlete. You've done better than a lot of the friends you had in elementary school and high school. But the progress you have made so far isn't permanent. Graduating from college is what will allow that progress to continue all through your life. Think about the people you know who were college athletes but came back to the neighborhood not much better off — except for some memories and stories — than when they left. They may have enjoyed fun and glory as athletes, but there was also a lot of pain and disappointment. Some of them are worse off than before they went to college, especially if they have no degree to show for the years they spent in school.

You don't want to end up being one of those who are used and abused: worse for the wear but no better for the experience of college sports. Don't just spend time in college being an athlete and hanging out. Spending time that way is wasting time.

Don't end up being one of those who are used and abused: worse for the wear but no better for the experience.

"We're becoming a nation which in the future will be divided along lines not of race but of education."[9] These words, from Harold Howe II, chairman of the Grant Foundation's Commission on Youth and America's Future, mean that your best chance to overcome racism is to have a college degree and a good job. Knowledge, a good income, a college degree, and high status are the things that give a person the power to make a good life. Discrimination still exists, but it will have much less effect on a person who is educated and has a degree to prove it.

Communication

Communication is a two-way street. It includes taking in what other people have to say (listening and reading) and letting other people know what you have to say (speaking and writing). Student-athletes who belong to minority groups often have difficulty with communication skills — speaking, writing, listening, and reading—as do many other students. Yet this is the most important set of skills you can improve in college. Good communication skills will make a big difference in the level of success you attain in your career. If your communication skills are limited, there is no way you can become a leader or be given much responsibility in your work. In fact, if you can't communicate well, you may not get a job in the first place.

In the job market, people are likely to hear you on the telephone or read your writing before they see you. Even if they see you first, that first impression will quickly be replaced by an opinion based on how well you express yourself and understand them.

Many people from minority groups have two ways of communicating: with the language they learned growing up and the one that is taught in school. The latter is the one used in most careers after college. You may feel at home with your first language—whether it's a black dialect, Spanish, or Asian—but you have to learn the official language if you want to succeed in college and in life afterward. That doesn't mean you have to give up the way you like to talk; you just have to learn the other to use in your career.

College, like the rest of life, is based on communication. If you are weak in reading and writing, take courses as soon as possible that will improve these skills. Devote time and effort to building these skills; the payoff will be greater than in any other area of schoolwork. You may forget a lot of what you learn in other courses, but once you improve your ability to write, read, and speak effectively, you will never lose it.

Even if you didn't read or write well in high school, you can develop these skills in college. Reading and writing abilities are not talents people are born with as some are born with the ability to be fast or to jump high. No one is born with the ability to communicate well.

Getting Help from Others

There are two kinds of help you can get: good help and bad help. And there are all kinds of people willing to give help, ranging from those who do it for your benefit to those who do it to serve their own needs. If someone shows you a better way to do something—that's helpful. If someone shows you how to avoid doing something—that's hurtful to you.

For example, let's say a tutor or an academic adviser shows you how to use a computer in the library to find references for a term paper. That kind of help may seem like a pain, but it's really helping you. Not only are you gaining knowledge and getting the term paper done, but you're also learning a skill that will be valuable in other classes and on the job after you graduate. In contrast, let's say a tutor or academic adviser (or someone else) shows you how to cut corners just to get the term paper over with. This may appear helpful because you really do want to get it over with, but it's hurting you. The difference between these two kinds of help is very much like working out. What hurts really helps. No pain, no gain.

Black basketball players in college report feeling forced into taking easier courses, fewer courses per term, and less demanding majors than white basketball players.

W. M. Leonard II [10]

More so than white athletes, black athletes attract people who come around to help by doing the schoolwork for them. Maybe these people feel that you can't do the work yourself and they want to help keep you eligible for sports. Keeping you eligible is all that is important to them. They don't care about your education. In fact, they are displaying their bigotry by assuming you can't get the work done yourself. They don't respect you enough to let you learn on your own.

A much better kind of help comes from people who show you how to accomplish all the tasks required of a good student. These helpers aren't interested in having you avoid your responsibility; they want you to get the job done, because that's the only way you'll learn to get jobs done once they are gone from your life.

Hang out with Friends Who Are on the Success Track

Regardless of race, some people in college are on the success track, while others are on the failure track. It is easy to spot the successes and the failures by what they do or don't do regarding schoolwork and by what they say to people who are striving for success.

Being a good student, going for grades, and wanting to graduate are referred to by some people as "acting white."[11] Because of this, some black students don't speak up in class, get lower grades than they are capable of, or hide their intelligence in other ways. Doing this, even to keep from losing face among your friends, is self-defeating. The result is a short-term gain but a serious long-term loss. White athletes also sometimes play dumb, but the problem is worse for black athletes because they also have to overcome bigotry.

The problem starts with the bigotry of whites who believe that blacks are not smart, but it comes full circle. Some blacks begin to believe that they aren't smart enough to succeed in college, or, perhaps, they just don't care about trying to do well in school. To make themselves feel better, they put down other blacks who are striving to succeed in academics. Thus, blacks who avoid "acting white" are making it easy for other people to think that blacks are not very smart after all. Not trying to do well in college in order to avoid "acting white" only harms you. It can destroy your chances for a good career after sports.

People want to be with others like themselves. Athletes like to hang out with other athletes. Blacks feel comfortable with other blacks. The same is true of Hispanics, Asians, Native Americans, and whites. Billy Mills, Olympic gold medalist in the 10,000-meter run at the Tokyo Olympics, was born to a Sioux Indian father and a white mother. He says he never felt accepted by either culture. "I found a third culture," he said. "Sports accepted me on equal terms."[12] It's natural to want to be with people like you who accept you.

There is nothing wrong about spending time with people you feel comfortable with — in fact, there is a lot right about it. But you should avoid spending time *only* with people like you. College is as much about growing and learning about other people as it is about the material in books and classes. College is the best and easiest time you will ever have to get to learn about people of other races and cultures and to become more comfortable with them. You will have to mix with other races after college, and it'll be much more difficult then if you haven't done it in college.

In addition, if you belong to only one group, it's easier to be influenced by peer pressure. Not all peer pressure is bad — there's pressure toward getting good grades, for example. But if it's negative peer pressure, such as pressure toward being a weak student (against getting good grades), then your group can bring you down.

Stereotypes

What would you think about a coach who gave a scholarship to a black athlete without seeing him or her perform because the coach assumed the athlete was quick and a good leaper? You'd think that coach wasn't too smart, even though many black athletes *are* quick and good leapers. The coach is guilty of stereotyping blacks — making blind judgments about individuals who happen to be members of a particular group. The coach could make the same mistake in assuming that a white athlete isn't fast and can't jump high.

The problem with stereotyping is that it's more often negative than positive. As mentioned earlier, some professors and even some coaches stereotype athletes as not being serious about school. Some people stereotype blacks in the same way. As such, the stereotype may be doubled for black athletes and be so apparent that some report that they feel it's harder for them to get good grades than it is for others.[13] Don't trap yourself into feeling that because you're black and an athlete, you can't be a good student. This kind of thinking will lead you to give up on yourself, and then you certainly won't do well in school. On the other hand, if you believe in yourself, you're more likely to do the things that lead to successful schoolwork. By doing those things — planning your time, discussing your progress and problems with professors, and letting them know well ahead of time about team trips — you're more likely to overcome the negative stereotype professors and coaches might have about you.

The Cold, Hard Realities of a Career in Professional Sports for Black Athletes

If you have the talent and the drive, aim for a career in professional sports. If you are motivated toward a sports career, more power to you. But in striving toward that goal, there are several things you should know.

Stacking in Professional Sports

Athletes are sometimes channeled into particular sports or playing positions based on their race and are discouraged from developing in other sports or positions. This is called "stacking." Stacking limits opportunities and can narrow a person's choices.

Why are there many more black wide receivers or running backs in football than there are quarterbacks or centers? In major-league baseball, 48 percent of the outfielders are black while only 5.1 percent of the pitchers and 4.4 percent of the catchers are black. More than one third (35.8 percent) of all major-league shortstops are Hispanic, but only 8 percent of first basemen and pitchers are Hispanic.[14] Stacking, whether deliberate or unintentional, is one explanation for these facts.

Black athletes have to work twice as hard and put up twice the numbers to get the attention that average white athletes get.

Robert Campbell, former student-athlete at
California State University, Sacramento [15]

Some people believe that members of various ethnic groups are naturals at some positions and not as good at others. The reality is that there have been great players from different ethnic groups at all positions. For example, Doug Williams, a black quarterback, led the Washington Redskins to a Super Bowl championship. The Seattle Seahawks' Steve Largent, who is white, is one of the greatest receivers of all time. Dwight Gooden of the New York Mets is better than the majority of white pitchers, while the Baltimore Orioles' Cal Ripken Jr., who is white, is a great shortstop, and the San Diego Padres' Benito Santiago, who is Hispanic, has been an All Star catcher.

Stacking occurs for several reasons. Those who control professional teams seem to believe that some ethnic groups are better at certain positions than at others. Sometimes, a coach will move a black player to a position he or she is better suited for — according to the coach—although that judgment may indicate the coach's bias more than it reflects truth. Also, young athletes will probably want to play the same position as their heroes. With few black professional quarterbacks, there are likely to be fewer black kids dreaming and striving to be quarterbacks than running backs or wide receivers. The same with pitchers in baseball. Of course, some black and Hispanic kids will want to play positions in which there are few heroes they can identify with, but more will want to play where their heroes play.

Stacking isn't as obvious in basketball because team leaders can be found at any position. But why aren't there more top-level black golfers and tennis players? Possibly because these sports cost more to play and much of the expense of training is borne by parents. But while there are black families that can afford the cost of training, there are very few role models for black youngsters in these sports. The 1989 women's professional tennis tour guide shows only two black players—Zina Garrison and Lori McNeil—in the top fifty, while France's Yannick Noah is the only black among the top fifty men players. In professional golf, the only black players among the more than 200 golfers listed in the 1989 *PGA Media Guide* were Calvin Peete and Jim Thorpe.

Four head coaching jobs recently were filled in the National Football League, and as usual, none of the new hires is black. The Jets, Cardinals, Oilers and Falcons interviewed more than 25 candidates, and a grand total of one was black.

John Sherlock in "What Hispanics Are Paid," *USA Today* [16]

Stacking causes several career problems for blacks. One problem is a shorter playing career, usually because the positions in which black athletes are stacked, such as running back or wide receiver in football, are prone to frequent injury. Another problem is that coaches tend to be drawn from positions played mostly by white players. This means that when a white athlete's playing career is over, he can more readily move into coaching, while black players generally have to find some other career. There has been only one black head coach in the National Football League, Art Shell of the Los Angeles Raiders, although more than half of the NFL players are black.[17] Further, when high-level coaching vacancies occur, black assistant coaches are bypassed in favor of white coaches who are recycled from other teams.

Major-league baseball in its entire history—more than 100 years—has seen only four black managers. And while 20 to 25 percent of the league's players are black, it wasn't until 1989 that two black managers opposed each other in a regular season game (the Baltimore Orioles' Frank Robinson and Cito Gaston of the Toronto Blue Jays). The NBA has had as many as five black head coaches at one time (out of twenty-seven teams), which, in comparison, seems better than the other pro sports. But more than three quarters of the NBA players are black, and it would seem that a greater number of black head coaches could be drawn from their ranks.

Why are there so few blacks in management and coaching positions? Because not enough people in power believe yet that blacks can lead a team.[18] Black athletes would be foolish to believe that there will be a career somewhere in pro sports for them after their playing career is over; as we've just pointed out, the chance of it happening is very small. This makes a convincing case that minority athletes need to prepare for some other career in case they don't succeed as a professional athlete or to fall back upon after their few years as a pro.

Rewards

Newspapers and magazines tell us about the big money that athletes earn, but how much do they really make in their athletics career? There is a lot of money to be made in pro sports, but relatively few athletes make enough to set themselves up for life. If you are a first- or second-round draft pick in football, basketball, or baseball, you will be very rich very quickly. About 160 athletes each year, *total*, in all three sports will make a lot of money upon signing their first contract. About half of them will be black or Hispanic. If you are one of these 80 athletes, good luck and we hope you find a competent and honest agent who won't cheat you out of your money. If you don't expect to be one of these 80, then you need to develop your plans for a career outside of athletics now.

Let's say you become a professional athlete. Let's also say you turn out to have enough talent and luck to last for the average professional career of four years. (Remember injuries. Remember competition from other athletes who are fighting for your roster slot or ranking and who think they are just as good as you.) In that time you will make between $600,000 and $2-million. It sounds like a lot of money, and it is. The problem is that professional athletes usually spend their earnings like a big timer and live high off the hog — a nice apartment in or near a big city (with high rent), good clothes and jewelry, and a classy car (at least one). Then there is the big bite that the tax people take. (If you play for a team in one state and live in another, you may have to pay taxes in two states.) Will your agent take care of your finances? A good one can help you hold on to some of that newfound wealth, but remember, an agent's fee amounts to a large slice of your money (off the top, before taxes).

In addition, if you make it big, you're certainly going to do something nice for the folks who raised you. Perhaps you'll buy them a new car or maybe even a new home. You can't forget your brothers and sisters, can you? And your friends will be hitting you up, since to them you're not only a big-time athlete, but a *rich* big-time athlete.

It may sound strange, but $2-million won't last long in that life-style, and, if you are making closer to the minimum — about $300,000 over four years — your money can disappear even faster.

When pro athletes can't play anymore or someone else comes along to take their place, the money stops — cold (unless the athlete's agent was smart enough to get a long-term payout). They don't get a pension when their career ends unless they've played for four or five years (depending on the sport). And if they do play long enough to collect a pension, they don't have access to it for at least twenty years. The minor sports leagues don't have pensions, and the salaries aren't enough to make ends meet out of season, much less make a player rich.

Even the big payoffs to the very best athletes are often not enough to sustain them. All college athletes should develop a nonsports career plan, so that their earning power will continue while life goes on.

71

Career Goals

One of the best things about being an athlete is that what's happening right now is important and fun. The payoff in schoolwork is somewhere down the road. In athletics, you work hard and don't have to wait long for the results. Coaches, teammates, other students, fans, and even some teachers can see the kind of effort you make and its outcome. While this "right now" focus feels good, it's one of the worst traps an athlete can fall into because it can lead you to avoid thinking about the future. As sure as day follows night, you can't be a college athlete forever. What are you going to do when you've played out your eligibility?

Spending four or five years in college playing ball and hoping for a career in pro basketball, football, baseball, tennis, golf, or whatever sport, is not developing a career. Harry Edwards points out that only about 1,200 blacks are employed in any capacity in professional sports. That includes all blacks who are pro athletes, coaches, sports journalists, or team staff. Every year thousands more black athletes come out of college hoping for one of those few jobs.

The black athlete who blindly sets out to fill the shoes of Dr. J., Reggie J., Magic J., Kareem-Abdul J., or O.J. may well end up with "No J." — no job that he is qualified to do in our modern, technologically sophisticated society.

Harry Edwards [19]

Why is it worse for black athletes than for white athletes? Because twice as many black football and basketball players as whites expect to become professional athletes. This means that more black athletes than whites have narrow, unrealistic career goals. We aren't saying that you should give up the dream of being a pro athlete, but rather that you must also prepare for a different career in case pro sports doesn't work out for you — for whatever reason. Even if you do earn a place on a pro roster, most rookies don't make it to a second season.

Have you been telling yourself that you'll take care of life after sports when it happens? Ask yourself about the likelihood of your returning to college to find a new career, especially without sports to make college fun and a scholarship to pay for it. Be realistic. You aren't likely to attend college a second time, so don't wait until after your playing days are over to find an alternative career.

Now is the time to look for a career that you might like — something in an area that you think will keep your interest for a long time. Find a career direction by talking to people who work in the jobs that interest you. Be curious about everything — the business world, working with children, health and fitness, law, college and university work, or the jobs held by your family members, parents of your friends, and other people you know. Which of these jobs do you believe that, with the right training or hands-on experience, you could do well in? Your college degree will give you the learning skills to do many different jobs successfully. Look into the fields that you feel fit you the best, and take full advantage of your strengths and personality.

6

Special Considerations for Women

Academic Performance . . . Title IX: Women's Rights and Opportunities in College Athletics . . . Publicity . . . Pressure . . . Sacrifice . . . Coaches: Male and Female . . . Physical Considerations . . . The Masculinity/Femininity Issue . . . Sexual Harassment . . . Careers in Sports . . . Nonplaying Careers in Sports

The following are facts about women in sports.

- Female athletes tend to perform better in academics in college than male athletes.
- Title IX has made it possible for women's sports to gain greater support.
- Publicity for women's sports teams is improving, although it is a two-edged sword.
- Female athletes do not yet experience as much competitive pressure as male athletes.
- There will be increasing demand for female coaches.
- Women are narrowing the performance gap in some sports between themselves and men.
- Sports can enhance rather than diminish a woman's femininity.

This chapter was written in consultation with Dr. Gail Whitaker of San Francisco State University. Professor Whitaker is coauthor of *Sport and Play in American Life* (Dubuque: Wm. C. Brown, 1991).

- Women are learning to be aggressive on and off the playing field without the negative connotation of that behavior.

- There are a growing number of sports-related career opportunities for women.

Currently, the situation in women's sports is good, and the future, although not completely rosy, looks even better. This chapter discusses what female athletes need to know and do in order to survive and thrive in college athletics. You want to enjoy your sports experience, grow as a person, and maximize your success in athletics, academics, and your eventual career.

Academic Performance

Overall, athletes are often stereotyped as dumb or at least not as academically motivated as other students. In most cases in which athletes do not perform well in academics, it is because of time commitments, the special pressures found in competition, and the negative influences that they encounter in their sports experiences. In spite of these, female athletes generally seem to be much more successful as students than their male counterparts. Female athletes tend to have a higher high school grade point average, spend an average of 5 more hours per week on college schoolwork, and have better study habits and skills than male athletes.[1]

Why is academic success more likely for women in sports than for men? Perhaps because women have fewer professional career opportunities in sports, they are more apt to focus on the schoolwork necessary to earn a degree in preparation for a nonplaying career. Another reason could be that women's collegiate athletics tends to be less pressurized than men's. Interestingly, the academic performance of female athletes has been known to decrease as the ranking and importance of their team grows.[2]

While the academic terrain for female athletes may be strewn with fewer hurdles, as a female athlete you need to keep a keen eye on your own path. An increased budget in your sport, for example, may seem like a boon. But you should expect to pay for it with greater demands on you and your teammates for time and more pressure to succeed. The price of meeting these demands is likely to be a decrease in the quality of your schoolwork and social life.

With escalated competitiveness, coaches are likely to bring in new recruits who may not be as committed academically as those for whom sports are merely one part of their college experience. This could change the general attitude of the team toward school-work — with those who care about college and who work for good grades becoming outsiders on their own team. If this happens, you'll need to dig deeper into your own resources to maintain your commitment to succeeding in academics.

[Female] basketball players and women with athletic grants in other sports come to college placing great importance on earning a college degree, and many are planning to attend graduate or professional schools.

NCAA News [3]

If a women's team models itself after a men's team and it aspires to a similar level of competition, then you can expect the athletes on that team will find increased pressure to slack off on their academic priorities. If you're on such a team, you have to resist this pressure in order to complete your degree and get the education and career benefits that you want. Being aware that you are being pressured in that way can keep you from falling into too deep an academic hole.

Title IX: Women's Rights and Opportunities in College Athletics

Title IX, a federal law enacted in 1972, states that:

> No person in the United States shall on the basis of sex be excluded from participation in, be denied the benefits of, or be subjected to discrimination under any educational program or activity receiving Federal financial assistance.

Your team probably owes its existence to Title IX. At the time that Title IX first became law, most college women interested in sports competition were limited to powder-puff games and play days. By 1988, however, colleges fielded an average of seven intercollegiate women's teams.[4] Before Title IX, no athletics scholarships were available to women.

As the law has come to be interpreted, schools are required to provide female athletes with athletics scholarships equivalent to the number provided for male athletes. For example, if a school has 200 male athletes and 100 of them get athletics grants, and that school has 100 female athletes, then at least 50 of the women must be awarded athletics grants. For other funding—money for traveling, equipment and uniforms, and practice facilities—Title IX calls for women's and men's teams to be treated equally.

Although Title IX doesn't directly mention athletics (it applies to *all* educational programs), it is responsible for the increased opportunities for women in athletics. Through the years, the scope of Title IX has been narrowed (as a result of the Grove City College case, 1984), then expanded again (through the Civil Rights Restoration Act, 1988).[5] In its current form, Title IX protects your rights to opportunities in school similar, if not identical, to those enjoyed by men.

But laws, like rules, are sometimes bent and broken. Lawsuits based on alleged Title IX violations have frequently been filed against schools by women who feel they haven't been given equal opportunity in athletics. How diligently Title IX is adhered to at a particular school depends on a combination of factors, including the amount of money available for athletics and the importance of equal opportunity in the eyes of school and government administrators. Title IX gives you rights under the law, but you may have to fight for those rights.

What might you be fighting for? As has been discussed, female athletes are entitled to a fair share of athletics resources. More basically, they are entitled to the opportunity to compete in sports. For example, if your school has a men's soccer team and there are enough women who want to participate in soccer, the school should either fund and form a women's team or open the men's team to women. To start a team under Title IX, proceed in the following way.

1. Find enough women (enough to field a team of starters and substitutes) who want to play the sport.
2. Approach the school athletics director with your request.
3. If the athletics director refuses to agree or to act on your request, contact the campus affirmative action officer and provide a detailed accounting of the steps you have taken to

that point, including names, dates, and copies of correspondence. (The affirmative action officer's name will be listed in the college catalog. If you can't find it there, call the main campus switchboard.) The affirmative action office exists specifically to ensure that the school complies with laws against any kind of discrimination based on sex, race, age, and disability. You have the right and perhaps even a responsibility to let the affirmative action office know when you feel that you've been discriminated against.

While the [Civil Rights] Restoration Act doesn't specifically address women's sports programs, one of its effects will be to give women seeking equal opportunity in athletics renewed legal clout.

Craig Neff in *Sports Illustrated* [6]

Publicity

Women's teams rarely get as much publicity as men's teams, and this can lead female athletes and their coaches to feel like second-class citizens. Championship women's teams may be largely ignored in the media, while losing men's teams at the same school may get publicity daily. This can happen in the same sport, especially in revenue-earning sports such as basketball. Your coach should make sure that the school's sports information director (SID) has constant and complete information about your team and the players. However, neither your coach nor the SID can force the local newspapers and broadcast media to report on your team.

It seems unfair that the media ignore women's sports, especially when teams are highly successful. But the media see their job as providing the public with what it wants and don't necessarily reward success with greater attention. As unfair as the lack of publicity may be, women's athletics may be better for it. Public attention to success generates pressure for more success, which leads to the kinds of abuses rampant in men's sports. Before settling your mind on the unfairness of being ignored, consider these two options: (1) clean, honest, and enjoyable athletics ignored by the public and (2) well-publicized athletics brimming with excesses and abuses — drugs, stacking, and gambling, to name a few.

You might ask, "Isn't it possible to have some of each — some publicity *and* a clean, enjoyable college athletics experience?" Perhaps, but publicity tends to breed the need for more publicity. Once athletes, coaches, and their schools get to the point of liking and expecting public exposure, it's hard to turn back. If you're at a college where the publicity your team receives is balanced nicely with the normal life of a college student, consider yourself lucky.

Pressure

Pressure for success in athletics can come from the general public or from within campus, or it can be imposed by an athlete herself. Your desire to achieve in sports may lead you to overlook or forgo other values. The pressure that coaches place on themselves often leads them to put pressure on their athletes, and sometimes that pressure is excessive.

Just as a certain amount of internal pressure is necessary to make engines run, a certain amount is needed to drive people to achieve. And, as too much pressure will cause an engine to break down, it will also cause a student-athlete to forget her reasons for being in school. It may lead her to not do the work it takes to achieve her goals.

As stated in Chapter 2, pressure to win, to gain a tournament invitation, or to earn a high ranking may be imposed upon the coach and athletes from outside sources. The greatest outside pressure imposed on a coach, of course, is a threat to his or her job. Fortunately, at this point in women's athletics, relatively few coaches are threatened with losing their job if they don't win championships or achieve a high ranking. The monetary costs of women's sports are low compared with those of men's sports (especially football), and even a highly successful women's team will earn relatively little money and publicity. It wasn't until 1988 that the entire NCAA Division I women's basketball tournament earned over $1-million. This may seem like a lot of money, but note that in the same year, more than $1-million was earned by *each* of the Final Four men's teams, while each Final Four women's team earned only $33,593 (less than 3 percent of comparable men's team earnings).[7] College officials and alumni and booster groups want women's teams to succeed, but there is little financial risk if they don't, so coaches of women's teams feel less threatened.

Nevertheless, abuses in women's intercollegiate athletics have been increasing as women's athletics programs come to resemble men's Division I programs more closely.[8] Female athletes in these programs tend to sacrifice schoolwork, take lighter course loads during terms when they are in competition, experience unrealistic demands on their time, and be more frequently asked to play while injured than women in less competitive programs. In general, female athletes also seem to be more preoccupied with their competition weight, which can lead to eating disorders, as well as to emotional manipulation and intimidation by coaches.

Now that there is enforcement from the NCAA, people are going to get caught cheating. The interest, money, and prestige put pressure on a coach to win.

Debbie Ryan, women's basketball coach,
University of Virginia [9]

Violations of NCAA regulations in women's programs have increased. When violations are found, the association can force the school to reduce the number of athletics scholarships available, teams can be banned from postseason competition, and athletes can lose their eligibility and grants. The NCAA imposed all of these penalties on Eastern Kentucky University in 1989, when the women's basketball coach was found to have illegally given cash, meals, clothing, and transportation to two players during recruitment and after enrollment.[10] While a coach may be fired as a result of an investigation (as happened to the coach at Eastern Kentucky), the punishments imposed on the program by the NCAA — banishment from tournaments and reduced scholarships — are felt by the athletes, including those who did nothing wrong. This isn't fair, but governing agencies such as the NCAA have yet to figure out a better way.

Sacrifice

Too often, success is the primary objective in men's athletics, and all other goals are sacrificed if they interfere with it. It hasn't always been that way in women's sports, but the differences between men's and women's athletics are becoming fewer. While men's athletics struggles to reduce the pressure and overemphasis on winning, women's athletics has just begun to experience similar pressures and the related excesses.

What can you do if you find yourself in a pressure-packed situation? First, be aware that there is a problem. Too often we don't face problems until we are half buried by them. Pressure in athletics and its effect on academic performance are like being caught in quicksand — the more immersed you get, the harder it is to reach solid ground. The answer (simply stated, though not easily done) is to keep a firm grasp on your long-term goals of career preparation and graduation. Don't allow yourself to get pulled so far down into the mire that you sacrifice your education in favor of short-term success in athletics.

[Female athletes] seem to be thinking of college more for the educational value than as an opportunity to develop sports skills. As a result, the women seem to come to college having developed better study habits and skills.

Robert A. Rossi,
American Institutes for Research [11]

Success in athletics need not come at the cost of academic success. In fact, the confidence, time management skills, and perseverance that can be developed in pursuit of sports success may lead to better grades and a more focused, goal-directed education. If you maintain the right attitude about your education and follow the suggestions in this book, the luxury of wasting time may be your greatest sacrifice. Athletes must be aware that some sacrifices are likely when one is committed to sports. The good news is that with planning you can often select what you will be sacrificing.

Coaches: Male and Female

Ironically, as women's intercollegiate athletics has grown, the proportion of female coaches has shrunk. In 1972, when Title IX first became law, 90 percent of women's teams were coached by females.[12] By 1988, less than half (48.3 percent) had female coaches. When men's and women's teams are both under one head coach — in swimming, for example — the coach is almost always male.[13]

Why are there so few female coaches? Any of the following beliefs or myths could explain it.

- Women are not competitive enough.
- Women never learned the motor skills required at current levels of women's competition.
- Women are not committed enough to sport and career to pay the price to achieve success.
- College coaches are hired through an old-boy network in which females are not accepted (84 percent of women's athletics programs are administered by men[14]).
- Female coaches are sometimes stereotyped as lesbians.

These beliefs or myths, sometimes held by athletics directors, may lead such directors to discriminate against women who apply for coaching jobs. But there are other, nondiscriminatory reasons that could also explain the low number of female coaches.

- As the publicity, status, and rewards in women's intercollegiate athletics increase, more men are attracted to the coaching positions.
- Some men are attracted to relatively less pressure-packed women's sports.
- Some female coaches are disenchanted with the new women's athletics that involves recruiting and scholarships, and they leave the profession.

Physical Considerations

For years women were thought to be weak physically and not tough enough for competition. We now know that if women were indeed too weak, it was from a lack of physical training and not their physiological makeup. Female athletes today are surpassing men's world records from just a few years ago. Rules excluded women from marathons until the mid-1970s, yet by the late 1980s the top female marathoners were narrowing the gap between themselves and the best male marathoners. With more competition among women, more years of training, and more role models, who can say whether or not women might some day run marathons as fast as men?

In some sports, women compete well directly against men, so why not try in others? Female jockeys already compete, with a weight differential handicap, against men. Mixed doubles in tennis pits two female-male teams against each other. A stroke or distance handicap could be used to facilitate women competing against men in golf, and female-male teams could conceivably compete in foursomes. A coed professional volleyball league existed for several years in the early 1980s, which makes intercollegiate coed volleyball within the realm of reason. (Lack of precedent and tight funding for sports are perhaps the chief barriers to coed teams.)

The differences between top female and male athletes are cultural in a lot of respects. In the past, women were told that sports [weren't] for them. It followed that they weren't offered the same athletic opportunities.

E. C. Frederick, director,
Exeter Research Laboratory,
Brentwood, New Hampshire [15]

We don't mean to imply that in all sports women will reach the same levels as men. Even with long-term and well-guided training, the top female athletes are likely to be about 5 to 10 percent smaller, lighter, slower, and less powerful than men. This would present a problem in some sports if the sexes were in direct competition—in Olympic wrestling, professional ice hockey, and major-league baseball, to name a few. Women *have* competed in ice hockey, baseball, and football leagues on a small scale, but the leagues were short-lived.

There are, however, myths and misinformation concerning women and sports that need to be corrected. When playing the same sport, such as basketball, women do not get injured more often than men, and the injuries they sustain are no more serious.[16] Yes, women have less mass to protect themselves, but consequently they also generate less momentum. As long as women are competing against one another and not against men, their injuries will be no more of a problem than injuries are for male athletes.

This is not to downplay the seriousness of injuries in women's sports. Injuries are likely to increase as the level of competition approaches that of men's sports. The point is, female athletes are no more vulnerable to injuries than men. Women can compete in certain sports even when pregnant, although they are advised to reduce their athletic activity as the pregnancy progresses.[17]

Hard physical training may lead to changes in a woman's menstrual cycle and can cause a temporary halt to menstruation. The stoppage is nature's way of shutting down one system while another is highly activated. The menstrual cycle will return when the athlete halts or reduces her strenuous training. Apart from the risk of injury, the only long-term physical effect of a female's involvement in sport is a healthy body. And these days, a fit, trim person with well-defined muscles is considered attractive. Unless steroids are used — especially in combination with extreme dieting and dehydration, as is done in bodybuilding to make a woman's muscles pop out — there is no cause for concern that a female athlete will look like a man.

Along with the problem of extreme dieting, the use of steroids by female athletes has become a problem in recent years. As with male athletes, some female athletes feel that they need the competitive edge provided by drugs, extreme dieting, and dehydration. Some coaches encourage, or simply do not discourage, these physically and psychologically harmful competitive tactics. The harm can be immediate in terms of increased susceptibility to injury. Long-term effects can range from glandular changes — particularly in the liver — to heart problems and to death. (See the chart in Chapter 4 that compares the side effects of steroid use by women and men.)

The Masculinity/Femininity Issue

Despite the increasing level of participation and growing acceptance of women in sports, female athletes may still face disapproval and suspicion. This is less true in sports that emphasize grace and beauty, such as gymnastics and diving, and those that do not include direct physical confrontation, such as golf. Physical contact in sports has long been considered by some to be unacceptable and even harmful for women. Thus, women who play softball, basketball, and soccer may find their femininity in question. But beyond sports, some people see the very acts of striving and achieving as unfeminine—a legacy that many women in science, law, medicine, and business also have to contend with.

Other people's biases can sting, but it's more devastating when a female athlete questions her own sense of self. Most important is how you feel about yourself and how you view and carry yourself. This can influence how others see you. The discussion that follows looks at the specific behaviors that some people consider inappropriate or unfeminine but that are required by sports.

Aggressiveness

No coach wants an athlete who is not aggressive—aggressiveness is an athletic behavior. But there are two kinds of aggressiveness, one that is based in anger (emotional reaction to a problem or frustration) and one that focuses on solving problems (also called assertiveness). Anger-related aggressiveness is more typically a male than a female behavior. The other kind of aggressiveness—problem solving—brings success in sports (and science, business, the arts, etc.) and is neither typically male nor female. Female athletes have no reason to feel that problem-solving aggressiveness is unfeminine.

Competitiveness

Competitiveness is another behavior that some people think of as unfeminine but is needed in sports . But consider dance. In it, many women vie for only a few positions. You can bet that they compete for those scarce jobs every bit as intensely as female athletes do for championships in track, golf, and tennis, but they do so without loss of femininity.

Until recently women have had fewer opportunities than men to compete in sports and in most other careers. This led to the mistaken belief that females were naturally less competitive. In the few cases in which women could compete, their rewards often were much less than men's, which reduced their incentive for committing to competition. As a result, female athletes and coaches tended to emphasize skill development and fun over winning.

But those were the old days. Today, with greater opportunity to compete and increased payoffs for winning, more women are involved in competition more intensively. Thus, the perception of competitiveness as being unfeminine is slowly disappearing. In today's world, assertiveness and competitiveness are considered characteristic of adult behavior, rather than particularly masculine or unfeminine.[18] These are the kinds of behaviors shown by high-achieving women — scientists as well as athletes.

Athlete Profile

Finding Challenges in Life After Competition

You think you have your life together, and then things come along and change it. I had been a world-class triathlete and two days after I came home from college (in 1985) to train for a triathlon in Nice, France, the front wheel came off my bicycle while I was riding and I did a face plant in the pavement that required a series of surgeries. Six months later my brother, Mark, who was retarded and had always been my inspiration during training, died. I did a lot of thinking about my own future and decided, with my father's support, to find a career that could keep me interested, excited, and challenged and would include sports in some way. I had been studying speech communication, but I decided to change my major to sports medicine.

School has never been easy for me because I am dyslexic, which means that I can't read fast and have a difficult time distinguishing between numbers and letters. But that isn't stopping me from taking premed courses. The sciences now fascinate me because I am applying them to the sports that I know and love. Challenges are what make life exciting and fun, like a game. The way I look at it, I'm building a career on my love of sports and training myself to do what I want to do in life, so how can I do anything but win?

—Shawn Wilson, triathlete

Sexual Harassment

Unwanted sexual advances toward women are a societal problem more than specifically a problem within women's athletics. The issue here is not heterosexuality or lesbianism. It is women as sexual victims. We are discussing it here because of the closeness of athletics teams, both in the great amount of time that team members and coaches spend together and in the emotional closeness that comes with sharing goals and intense effort.[19] This doesn't mean that sexual harassment will necessarily be a problem on your team, but, if the situation occurs, you should know what you can do about it and know your rights.

How do you deal with an unwanted sexual advance? If it comes from a teammate, it's an interpersonal problem. Deal with it the same way you would handle an unwanted advance from a man—with a polite but firm rejection that doesn't attack the other person's ego.

Any sexual advance by a coach toward a student-athlete is unethical because the coach holds a position of greater power and control and because it is a violation of trust. You should be aware that a sexual advance from a coach or professor (male or female) may also be a violation of state law or university rules. Where such laws and rules exist, the coach or professor could lose his or her job—whether or not you welcome the relationship.

As with other interpersonal problems, the best way to deal with an advance by a coach is directly. Tell the coach you're not interested. Does this solution seem easier said than done? After all, the coach controls so much that is important to you: your access to competition, your place on the team, and even your scholarship. But when you weigh what is at stake—your control over your own body—self-respect must take precedence over any aspirations in athletics.

It would be normal for you to prefer avoiding a confrontation with the coach—if only to retain your place on the team. You might hope or wish that the problem will just go away, but it won't. The best way to make it go away is to deal with it directly with straightforward communication. Most coaches will stop their advances if you meet with them confidentially, indicate that you respect their needs, but reaffirm that you're not interested. As difficult as this might be, it's easier to do than the next acceptable alternative (assuming that quitting the team is not acceptable), which is filing a sexual harassment charge with the campus affirmative action office, the place where sexual harassment cases usually are handled.

For your own protection, it may be necessary to file sexual harassment charges, and, in doing so, you may feel that you're jeopardizing your position on the team and your relationship with teammates and friends. Fighting for your rights takes courage. If you do *not* deal with this problem, the problem will not only continue, but it will be a problem for other female athletes.

Careers in Sports

Female athletes have fewer opportunities for professional playing careers than male athletes. While golfers, skiers, and tennis players can aim toward professional circuits, as stated earlier, women's professional basketball, softball, and volleyball leagues have come and gone. Unfortunately, even in the best of those leagues, the pay was little more than a college graduate would earn as a beginning teacher — and teachers enjoy more job security and longer careers. Even professional golf and tennis, with six-figure tournament prizes, offer meager career opportunities. Only about 150 women tennis players in the entire world collect prize money equal to a beginning teacher's salary, and only about one third of those are Americans.[20] A career in professional golf, tennis, or skiing is a legitimate goal to aim for, but the odds of earning significant money are very small.

Title IX addresses fair opportunity for females in educational settings and doesn't cover professional sports. Professional leagues and circuits exist or die on market principles rather than on fair and equal opportunity. If the public is unwilling to support women's sports leagues, as has been the case so far, then career opportunities for top-level female college players in those sports don't exist.

Nonplaying Careers in Sports

High school or college coaching is a realistic opportunity for females who want a career in sports. We discussed earlier the decline in proportion of women coaches and administrators, but, as the number of women's teams increases as both Title IX and affirmative action are more firmly applied, the opportunities for females in coaching should increase dramatically. Other viable nonplaying career opportunities can be found in athletics training and sports medicine, both of which have already attracted a growing number of female athletes. And, in recent years, the number of females in sports journalism—on television and in newspapers and magazines—has risen from none to a few.

Women who want careers in sports are often pioneers, and pioneers by nature are willing to take chances. In addition to the careers already noted, good opportunities exist for women as athletics advisers, sports nutritionists, physical education teachers, sports promoters and managers, sports scientists, sports statisticians, and health club managers, among others. Chapter 10, "Careers in and out of Sports," gives more information about how to tie your interest in sports to your life beyond college.

7

Avoiding Exploitation

Who Is Responsible When Athletes Don't Get Their Fair Share? . . . Signs of Trouble: How to Tell if You Are Being Exploited

Among the most publicized and troubling examples of student-athletes whose college careers were thrown completely off balance by sports is Kevin Ross. Kevin, like too many other excellent athletes, allowed himself to go lightly on academics and devote himself almost entirely to his sport. In the process, he not only failed to get a college education but even failed to realize he needed extra help to do college-level work. Here is Kevin's story, as reported in the *Chicago Sun-Times*.

College Cage Star Joins Marva's 7th Grade

College basketball player Kevin Ross, who's 23 and 6 feet 9 inches tall, started class this week with seventh- and eighth-graders.

He has just spent four years at Creighton University in Omaha on an athletic scholarship without getting a degree, and he's intent on learning the basics that he somehow missed in high school and college.

Ross is quite talented at basketball, a captain of the team, but he wasn't wooed by the pros. And he has a clear-eyed determination to be ready academically for whatever life brings.

"I'm here to catch up," Ross said.

"My reading is about 65 percent, my spelling is about 40 percent. And reading comprehension, I can't get a percentage on.

"I just wish people in education would make sure students get an education."

Creighton officials said they agree with Ross on that.

Creighton is paying for his stay at Marva Collins' Westside Preparatory School, and athletic director Dan Offenburger went to Chicago today to help Ross find a place to live.

"We strongly encouraged Kevin" to attend Westside Prep, said Offenburger. "But basically it came down to Kevin accepting the challenge. He is a pioneer student, a 23-year-old man studying with grammar school and junior high kids."

Ross still wants to be a teacher, as he did when he entered Creighton.

Ross said he's considering looking for a job so he can afford to stay here. But Offenburger said that may not be necessary. "We found the (Creighton) stipend is sufficient in Omaha but not sufficient in Chicago. I've just got to get out in the streets with him and find a place for him to live. We're looking to schools or churches or private individuals."

Before Ross enrolled at Westside Prep, Creighton arranged for him and his mother to visit the school. Ross's mother, Opal Ross of Kansas City, Kan., is a postal worker who reared six children. Ross is her youngest. One of his sisters is a college graduate and pharmacist.

"I first heard of Westside Prep on TV," Ross said. The private school has 244 students, was founded by Collins, and is in its eighth year. It is basically for preschoolers through eighth-graders.

Collins, a former Chicago public school teacher, gained a national reputation for teaching youngsters who had been given up for lost educationally.

Ross's education deficit apparently started early. He was an "all everything" at sports at Wyandotte High School in Kansas City, where he finished 10th, 11th and 12th grades.

He feels he did not get a good education at Wyandotte. "Only once did a teacher lay it on the line and give me 5 — that's like an F — in class. And a coach taught me two other classes. I'd get A's and B's in them.

"When I got out of high school, I had a 2.0 grade average, which is what you've got to have to get into Creighton."

When Ross was recruited by Creighton, he said, "they told me 'You're going to be starting (at basketball), you're going to get your degree.

"All those school years, I gave 150 percent in basketball and I got 50 percent of an education."

His first two years at Creighton, Ross said, "I took courses that were not required for my major, a lot of Mickey Mouse courses, Ceramics, Introduction to Football."

But Offenburger said, "I would hate to see us look bad" on that. "With the dean's approval, we arranged, as we do for many students with particular problems, a lighter load in number of hours and types of courses."

When Ross finished his junior year, he said he felt "they were just trying to keep me eligible for basketball. And I was a good jumper and scorer."

Offenburger said, "Midway in his career, we found he had some difficulty with advanced courses in the curriculum. We worked with him through a special testing service in the summertime two years ago at the University of Missouri–Kansas City."

Ross was a forward and center on Creighton's Bluejays, and a captain.

In Ross' junior year, when Tom Apke was coach, the Bluejays won 21 and lost 9. In his senior year, former Knickerbocker star Willis Reed became coach and the team won 7 and lost 20.

Ross felt things changed for him with Reed as coach. "In the next to the last game, everybody played but me," he said. "I was captain but I was getting a backseat. And my worst grade card was in my senior year. My best were as a freshman and sophomore."

Offenburger said Creighton offered to pay for Westside.

"I think we've been working the last two years to best figure out how best to meet our obligations to Kevin," Offenburger said.

Ross said he is determined to stick it out at Westside Prep the full academic year.

Collins called Ross's motives in joining Westside Prep "very admirable" and added that "he hopes to make up in one year what he wasn't able to do in four years."

Kevin Ross's dismal educational experience as a college athlete sounds extreme, but it's not all that unusual. More than a few athletes spend four years in college with little to show for it but memories and a few stray credits. For instance, Dexter Manley, the Washington Redskins All Pro lineman, testified before Congress that he spent four years in college and still could not read.[1]

Where Kevin's case becomes unusual is in the help that people at Creighton and elsewhere gave him *after* his four years of playing eligibility expired. Although Kevin could no longer play basketball, Creighton, to its credit, extended his scholarship for another year and encouraged him to go back to junior high school to pick up the basic skills that he had somehow missed his first time around. To Kevin's credit, he agreed. Only a person with an uncommonly strong drive to learn and to grow, along with the personal strength to ignore ridicule, could have done this. Needless to say, most athletes who have been cheated out of their education just accept their fate as "the way it is" and fail to recover their lost education — ever.

Kevin Ross graduated from Westside Preparatory School at the age of 24. He said, "I just couldn't wait for the pearls to come falling through the ceiling. I did something and I feel a lot better about myself."[2]

Who Is Responsible When Athletes Don't Get Their Fair Share?

Dan Offenburger, former athletics director at Creighton, was concerned about Kevin Ross and what he represents in college sports. Offenburger wonders where the blame lies.

> The system failed him, Kevin failed the system (presumably by going along with it), maybe his mother failed him, maybe I failed him. But does the school get 60 percent of the blame, the mother 30, the high school 10? I mean, how do you assess who's to blame? [3]

Knowing who is responsible for an athlete's getting a good education is far more important than assigning blame for a bad one. The athletes themselves must keep alert that they as students are headed in the right direction, but their parents and coaches must stay on top of it too. Unfortunately, parents are often seen as intruders in the relationship between coaches and athletes. Parents sometimes even see themselves in this light and avoid becoming involved. But it is clearly the right and responsibility of all parents to be aware of what is occurring in their children's education, including the athletics part. The trick is for parents to approach their sons and daughters and their coaches in a concerned, inquisitive way rather than in a challenging way. A coach who has nothing to hide is likely to welcome parents who inquire about their child's performance in school and request the facts about his or her progress toward a degree.

Many high school and college coaches want to be concerned with the overall welfare, growth, and progress of their student-athletes. But in reality, coaches have to weigh those concerns against the task that keeps them in their job, namely, building and running a competitive and profitable athletics program. When one concern—the long-term welfare of athletes—is weighed against the other—producing a winning team and, in the process, ensuring their own job security—the latter often tips the scale.

Responsibility for the athlete's welfare is primarily up to the athlete. Knowing that coaches often face intense pressures to produce winning teams should give you incentive to protect yourself. The plight of Kevin Ross illustrates only too well that you can't count on anyone else to look out for your academic interests.

Signs of Trouble: How to Tell if You Are Being Exploited

It is likely you are being exploited if any one of the following situations occurs while you are a student-athlete.

- You are majoring in a field that someone else urged you into; it was not the one you wanted.
- You are taking nothing but easy courses in order to remain eligible for sports. This is called majoring in eligibility.
- You are being assigned to courses with other athletes, mainly to keep you together.
- Coaches and others advise you not to socialize with nonathletes.
- You accept the coach's suggestion, which you take to be a direct order, to take a summer job that will build your body, when you'd rather take a job that helps your major or career plans.
- The team demands so much of your time that you cannot perform your best in courses that you want or need for your future.
- Coaches steer you into courses that are easy but less valuable for your future and that won't take time and energy away from your team commitments.
- Coaches arrange aspects of your life (such as meals, housing, or leisure activities) so that you will interact primarily with other athletes and thus be more completely under the control of the coaching staff.

- Coaches tell you not to worry about taking courses now that will help you with your career. They say that they'll "get you a job" when that time comes.
- You are far more concerned about your success on the playing field than you are about the progress you are making toward your college degree.

Kevin Ross was passing classes; he just wasn't learning anything. If he had it to do over, only Kevin himself could have made the situation any different. Only he knew how little he was progressing as a student.

Passing only the minimum number of units necessary to stay eligible for sports doesn't "take care of business." Your business as a student is to get a good education, the kind that will help you thrive in the world after college and athletics. To take care of your educational business, you need:

1. More than 12 units each term in order to graduate in a reasonable amount of time and before your funds (whether the money comes from a scholarship, a loan, or your parents) dry up.
2. The *right* classes (i.e., meaningful and useful ones that make you struggle and stretch your abilities, not those that provide easy grades).
3. Courses that fit into your degree program.

Brian Rahilly, a college basketball player from the Midwest, had nearly all decisions made for him by his coaches. "I trusted these guys and said, 'Okay, I'll put my faith in you.' I was shortchanged."

Ted Gup in *Time* [4]

Whether or not you face the problem of exploitation (having your services as an athlete used without getting fair educational value in return) largely depends on the attitude of your college and coach. Some top-level athletics programs provide student-athletes with excellent educational and career opportunities. If you are in this situation, count yourself lucky and make the most of it. But other top-ranking programs, as well as some small-time programs, are concerned only with producing winning teams. They drain all that they can from their athletes, with little or no concern for the athletes' education and future. In this situation, the only two alternatives available if you don't want to sacrifice your education are to quit the team or transfer to another school.

Another situation is the coach's putting pressure on you to devote so much time and energy to your sport that your academic progress suffers. The coach may not realize that this is happening to you, nor might he or she intend it to happen. This is probably the most common situation. Fortunately, there are a number of things an athlete can do to correct this predicament. But first, how can you tell if you need to do anything?

The following imaginary scenarios mirror real situations that you may find yourself in. Each is followed by a likely (and harmful) result.

Scenario: All Billy Joe has ever wanted is to be an athlete. He doesn't really care about his education; instead, he is just happy to be a college athlete. The coaching staff is all too happy to have Billy Joe be nothing more than an athlete and devote all his time to training. They are "taking care of him" — but the few times he goes to class, he realizes how much more everyone else knows.

Result: Billy Joe may be given a diploma someday, but it won't be worth much. Even if he gets through a job interview and is hired, Billy Joe won't last long, because in the world of work, employers don't tolerate dead weight. Billy Joe may not even be able to get a job as a truck driver because the employer will wonder why someone with a college degree wants to drive a truck for a living.

Scenario: Bubba is staying eligible for sports, but he has been avoiding all the tough classes he'll have to take to graduate. He plans to take them after his eligibility expires, when he can devote more time to such classes. Coach told him to do this and it sounded pretty reasonable, especially when Coach said he would try to extend Bubba's scholarship or find him a job to help him through that extra year or two of school. "One thing at a time," Coach always says.

Result: Bubba can't handle all those tough classes at once, especially after having taken easy ones for four years. Bubba hung it up and decided a college degree wasn't worth the effort anyway.

Scenario: Barbara competed for four years, used up her eligibility, and then dropped out of school lacking about a year's worth of credits for graduation. She just got tired of being in school. She thought that maybe after working for a year or two, she would return and finish her degree. That was five years ago.

Result: Barbara probably won't ever return to school. Tuition is higher now and the longer she waits, the more she is likely to be intimidated by professors, other students, the loss of her study skills, computers, and whatever else is new on the college scene. Waitresses can earn a good living, but work conditions aren't the greatest and there isn't much room for advancement.

Scenario: Betty Lou cares about getting an education, but her coach demands so much time that she can't give all she would like to her schoolwork. In fact, the coach has tried to advise her against taking a couple of tough courses that would help her get into graduate school. ("Part of the price you pay for being an athlete," the coach said.) Betty Lou took the courses anyway (risking her coach's wrath) but didn't do well since she couldn't devote enough time to them because of team commitments.

Result: Betty Lou got into graduate school (although not the one she wanted) but is struggling to keep up with the students who understand the material she didn't learn in her undergraduate major. In graduate school there is no time to go back and learn the basics, especially for Betty Lou, since she also has to hold down a part-time job to make ends meet. In addition, graduate schools require that students maintain at least a B average. Betty Lou is considering dropping out before they kick her out.

Scenario: Bruce's friend Bart did only what was necessary to stay eligible for sports, then dropped out of school and is now making a lot of money at a pretty good job. Bruce looks at Bart's life and wonders what's so all-fired necessary about making sure he gets a good and complete college education.

Result: For every Bart you hear about, there are twenty you don't hear about who are pushing a broom, driving a taxi, or selling used cars.

College athletes are also capable of treating themselves unfairly, engaging in a kind of self-exploitation. They often feel torn in two when having to decide between athletics needs and interests and their academic responsibilities and goals. It's very tempting to take the easy way out and put off your academic responsibilities until some later time. Whether you postpone tasks for a given class or avoid your responsibilities for your entire degree and career plans, any delay in taking care of academic responsibilities makes it more difficult to take care of them in the future. If you get into this bad habit of taking care of sports now and academics later, you are almost guaranteed to be exploiting yourself. You will end up being the loser. If this happens, you can't blame anyone else. You will have done it to yourself.

Grant Darkow majored in biology and played linebacker for the University of Missouri. Honored as an Academic All-America, Darkow believes that the people who run college athletics programs have a responsibility to their student-athletes. Focusing on football, he said:

> So many kids are going to college who have their hearts set on playing pro football but end up just being used. When they get through, what have they got if they didn't study? It's not only the responsibility of the student to study and get a degree, but it's also the responsibility of the administrators and the coaches to see he doesn't waste his time there and gets an education as well as the experience of being an athlete.[5]

Profile of a Star Running Back About to Go Down the Tubes
(with a little help from his "friends")

Net yards gained in college career . . . . 3,000+

Seasons awarded "All-Conference" honor 2

Semesters spent in college 7

Semesters of varsity competition . . . . . . 6 (4 in football, 2 in track)

Semesters on academic probation
or disqualified and reinstated 4

Total semester credits earned to
date . . . . 86 (total needed to graduate: 126)

Credits earned toward
GE requirements . . . . 31 (total needed to graduate: 46)

Credits earned toward
business major . . . . 3 (total needed to graduate: 60)

Minimum additional semesters needed to graduate
(based on a normal course load) 5

Overall grade point average 2.09

GPA in phys. ed. activities and athletics courses 3.29

GPA in all other courses 1.42

Note: This athlete was told by his coaches and others that he could expect to be a high draft choice in the NFL. However, the colleges against whom he starred were not big-time caliber and his own school had not placed a single player in the NFL during the previous ten years. Yet, it looks as if this athlete put all of his efforts into that one dream. What would he do if he didn't make it in football? (He did make it to the NFL but lasted only one season playing on a kick-return squad.)

It may seem that at times in this chapter we've painted a bleak picture of college athletics, in which athletes invariably are forced to battle the system if they really want an education. In fact, at many schools that is just how it was for many years — and still is. But you are fortunate in that those who run college athletics programs, from coaches to administrators to national college athletics associations, are becoming increasingly aware and concerned about athletes getting a fair chance at receiving a solid, well-rounded education and strong preparation for a career. As a result, the administrators and sports personnel you deal with are more likely to encourage and support you in these pursuits now than they did in the past.

I was greased all the way through high school; they'll grease me through here.

Carl Hayes, college basketball player [6]

If you stand up for your rights as a student, your chances of getting all that should be coming your way in terms of a college education are better today than they were for athletes in the past. Being an athlete no longer necessarily means sacrificing important parts of your education. But the responsibility to make the system work for you is yours. It's up to you to get the full rewards of college in return for the extra effort that coaches expect from you as an athlete.

8

Academic Cross-Training

*Fighting the Dumb-Jock Image . . .
How to Be an Active Student . . . Time
Management: The Critical Skill for
Student-Athletes . . . Improving the Learning
Skills Needed for College-Level Work . . . How to
Handle Test Anxiety . . . How to Respond to
Poor Performance . . . The Academic Pie*

Any athlete can be a successful student by organizing time, apply-ing effective study skills, and taking advantage of help that is available on the campus. The rigors of athletic training make stu-dent life more difficult for student-athletes, but athletes are also tougher than the average student. The student-athlete can be just as intensely goal directed about studies as about sports. The first hurdle to cross when striving to become a successful student is to believe in oneself.

Fighting the Dumb-Jock Image

Unfortunately, athletes aren't always judged on their own mer-its. As was discussed in Chapter 2, the image of athletes as dumb jocks is held by some teachers, some students, and—worst of all—by some athletes. It suggests that if you are an athlete, you are probably less able to do college-level work than other students. Further, the dumb-jock image suggests that you probably aren't interested in schoolwork even if you have the ability.

The dumb-jock image exists to one degree or another on most college campuses. Sometimes this reputation is earned; at other times, athletes are stereotyped in this way as a result of jealousy on the part of those who wish they had some of the attention that athletes enjoy.

The real problem with the dumb-jock image lies among athletes themselves, especially when being a good student is considered uncool.

J oke circulating on college campuses:
"How many college athletes does it take to change a light bulb?"
"I don't know, but they all get 3 units of course credit."

You may find a few teammates, some of whom might even be among the leading players, who seem to take pride in avoiding schoolwork: they don't study, fail to meet deadlines, and try to get around regulations. They don't want to do well in school. Whether this behavior is from lack of ability or lack of interest doesn't really matter. What matters is that these individuals seem to feel better about themselves if they can get their teammates to behave in the same uninterested, negative way about academics. For them, it's a source of pride that they neither know nor care about good study habits. They believe that the coach or someone else will always take care of them.

Athletes who behave this way only help to sustain the dumb-jock image. This is why we say that, in some cases, the image is earned. It is a trap that you may fall into, especially if you take the wrong team leaders as your model. Once you've chosen the dumb-jock image for yourself, you'll have a hard, though not impossible, time shedding it.

Our best advice here is to be an individual in your schoolwork and be a teammate on your team. This isn't easy. You are both a student and an athlete, but you *may* have to act differently in each situation to feel as if you fit in.

If you were admitted to college, you are probably as bright as most other students and capable of doing college-level work. Of course, everyone knows that some athletes are admitted to college because of their good athletic skills and in spite of their poor academic skills. Athletes admitted to college on this basis are often called "special admissions." First, you must decide whether this is actually your situation or whether you are simply carrying the common (but unfounded) newcomers' feeling that everyone else is smarter. If you are a special admit or if you find from test or writing scores (after giving them a good, honest try) that other students seem to be better than you, you *must* seek extra help. (Refer to Chapter 3 for sources of academic assistance.)

How to Be an Active Student

You'll enjoy your education more by being an active participant. It may seem as if the easy way through college is to walk into your classrooms, hide in the back, keep your mouth and mind shut, and do the least work that you possibly can to get by with a decent grade. Actually, this is the hard way, because it makes attending classes drudgery and you'll tend to either rush through your assignments the night before they are due or forget to do them altogether. Students who take this approach look for excuses to avoid attending classes and gain virtually nothing from their assignments but an intense dislike of their academic responsibilities. This negative behavior pattern is too often carried over into one's work career. This is definitely *not* the easy nor the enjoyable way to get through college.

There are specific things that you can do in order to enjoy and benefit from college classes. But you must *choose* to do these things; they won't happen on their own.

Set Goals

Set long-term general goals for yourself as well as short-term specific goals. Don't take a course just because it's required or because it fits into your schedule. Decide at the beginning what you want to gain from it. Decide before you begin a class project or a reading assignment what you want to gain from it. Write your goal on a piece of paper and then, after the task is completed, check to see that your goal was accomplished. Setting goals and keeping them in mind help to keep you alert and in tune to what you are doing; they also help you avoid wasting time. The examples cited here should give you an idea of how simple — yet worthwhile — goal setting can be.

- *Goal for a general education course on computers and society:* To see if I have the interest and ability to take a major in computer science.

- *Goal for a course in conversational Spanish:* To learn to speak Spanish well enough to carry on a one-hour conversation with a Spanish-speaking person who doesn't know English so I can travel in Spain or South America.

- *Goal for a sociology term paper:* To find out how many college basketball coaches at major universities have earned a master's degree in the past ten years. (Part of a larger goal: to explore the occupation of college coach.)

Set short-term and long-term goals in your schoolwork as you do in sports.

Speak Up, Question

Speak your mind in class whenever class size and instructor's style permit, and certainly speak up out of class as well. College is the perfect time and place to try out new ideas and measure your beliefs against the beliefs of others. College is meant for trying out different ways of thinking and acting. Open your mind to the ideas of others. Student bull sessions can be valuable and enjoyable learning tools. If you don't involve yourself, you run the risk of making yourself an outsider among other college students.

Question What You Read

The author of a book or article may not be available to you, but a professor who is knowledgeable in the area *is*. One of the best, most valuable parts of a college education is the constant give-and-take among faculty and students on the assigned readings and on reading matter in general.

Open Your Mind to Learning All the Time

Learning habits, like athletic habits, generate their own momentum. A well-trained athlete enjoys training and finds it easy to continue training. A poorly trained athlete, especially one who cuts corners, considers training to be drudgery and finds excuses to avoid it. The same patterns apply to learning.

Does this mean that you have to crack the books all the time? No. It simply means you should also consider the time you spend outside of class and away from assigned readings to be valuable learning time. The content of all classes, from quantum physics to business law to English 1A, has an application in the real world. Archimedes discovered the law of specific gravity while watching water spill over the side as he sat in his bathtub. This is a classic example of learning in a setting different from the environment where you expect to learn (the classroom, the laboratory, etc.).

Work at Making Yourself Understood

If you don't know what you are saying, no one else will. People who fill their sentences with several "you know"s may be copping extra time to gather their thoughts, but they are also sending their listener a signal that really says, "I hope you understand what I can't say very well."

No one is expected to know all things. But we all can improve the way we communicate what we know and don't know. Keep a dictionary handy whenever you study, read, or write. It's even a good practice to take a pocket dictionary to class, so you can quickly define words you aren't sure of and thus gain more from the class. College is for learning new things, *not* for hiding what you don't know.

Paraphrase to Learn

Asking "What does that mean?" simply but effectively puts you in the position of stating a thought in different words, that is, *paraphrasing*. If you can put a thought accurately into different words, that thought has been understood. The words are no longer abstractions or just words. Instead, they now create a picture in your mind that you can look at, analyze, and understand better.

By asking "What does that mean?" of your reading and then paraphrasing the answer, you'll understand more from reading something *one time* than most others would from reading it several times. So, while it may seem that paraphrasing slows you down, it's actually quicker in the long run, and you'll understand and retain more of what you read. A little investment now, a big payoff later.

When a point is made in class, ask yourself, "What does that mean?" If you can't come up with a clear answer, take the next step and ask the professor for clarification. If you find yourself doing this a lot in a particular class, or if you find that the professor doesn't like to be interrupted, write a note to yourself to ask another student or the teaching assistant outside of class. If you still can't get a satisfactory answer, go to the professor during office hours or after a class session and ask for an explanation of the point that isn't clear to you. The professor is likely to paraphrase for you. Hearing the same idea or information expressed two different ways is an excellent strategy for gaining an understanding of it, whether you or someone else does the paraphrasing.

As a bonus, you may find that talking with the professor outside of class gives you much more useful information than simply clarifying the point that you didn't understand. Professors like to see students show interest in their subject matter, and they will often go out of their way to help interested students do well.

Learn to Listen

As a child, you may have heard the old saying "You can learn more by listening than by talking." Listening is a skill that most of us could develop much more fully. Often, we are so busy thinking about what to say next or questioning other people's motives that we fail to hear what they are saying. It's likely that more arguments occur because people misunderstand one another than for any other reason.

Improving your listening habits has benefits beyond the classroom. People respond well to someone who really listens to them. Good listeners are often considered very bright, even without saying anything especially bright. Looking directly at the speaker — without staring — creates a very good impression and also helps you to absorb information and ideas.

Listen. Hear what others are saying. College isn't necessarily for changing your mind, but it *is* for opening it.

In listening to professors and others, you are likely to hear things you don't agree with. Resist the temptation to say so or to discard their message simply because you disagree. Try their thoughts on for size, even though you initially disagree. Try to see where they might be right and you might be wrong. College isn't necessarily for changing your mind, but it is for *opening* it. Good listening skills may be the best tools of all for accomplishing that.

Time Management: The Critical Skill for Student-Athletes

Managing your time efficiently may be the hardest task you face in college. It is a task that will remain difficult as long as you combine athletic and academic pursuits. All good students have to work at efficient use of their time, but athletes need to be even better at it than most students because athletic and academic responsibilities represent two full-time jobs. You may know some student-athletes who seem to float through college playing cards, tossing Frisbees, telling jokes, and generally playing around. They exist on every campus and are often popular because they are always available to socialize with. But such individuals are not good role models for several reasons. First, they are usually in more hot water than they are willing to admit. Wasting time is often their way of saying, "I can't hack it, so I don't really care." Second, beneath the fun-loving image you'll probably find a person who is heading down a dead-end street. These people may have a lot of natural talent, but they are wasting it by not working to develop it further. Others who begin with less but are willing to put in the time to develop their talents are likely to pass them by, both in college and in the job market. Third, student-athletes who have a habit of wasting time are looking for others whom they can drag down to their level. If you see three athletes who tend to waste time, you could make a nice profit betting that two of them will flunk out, drop out, or at least lose their eligibility.

Scheduling Your Time

Making good use of your time requires effort, practice, and vigilance, and it will make college life far more enjoyable and profitable for you. The basic strategy is simple enough: prepare a weekly activities calendar and follow it religiously. Keep your calendar accessible; it does little good inside your desk drawer. Tape it to the inside cover of your notebook. Fill out a new one every Sunday night *before* you begin that evening's study session. (If you wait until after the study session, you may be too tired or forget.)

The first items to fill in on your weekly calendar are class sessions. (As soon as you know your class schedule and fill it into the schedule, make a photocopy for each week in the term.) Next, fill in team practices, games, and travel. These are the commitments around which everything else in your week will revolve. If it is your sport's off-season, fill in time for conditioning and self-directed practice. If you have a part-time job, your work schedule must also be filled in. Don't forget to include sleep and eating time. Although these may be flexible, they take up significant blocks of time each day, so they should appear before you fill in time for studies, fun, and personal chores (laundry, shopping, etc.). Don't forget to schedule time for socializing. To keep efficient at work tasks, you need to relax and socialize, and you'll be able to enjoy this time more without feeling guilty about having fun if you include it as part of your schedule. And finally, take the effort to adjust and refine your schedule so that it's an accurate reflection of your week's activities.

A sample week's schedule is located on pages 112–13. A blank schedule has been provided on the two subsequent pages for you to photocopy and fill in for your own use.

Juggling Your Commitments

We are all created equal in at least one sense: every one of us has no more or less than 168 hours at our disposal each week. The difference is in how we spend our time. Consider the following.

- A normal semester course load is 15 units, which equals 15 hours in class each week.

- The rule of thumb for college courses is that 3 hours of study should be spent for every hour in class. This equals 45 hours of study each week.

- College athletes often spend 40 to 50 hours each week in such sport-connected activities as practice, games, travel, skull sessions, and conditioning.

- The total of the weekly time commitments listed above is 110 hours, which leaves only about 58 hours (roughly 8 hours per day) for *all* other activities (sleeping, eating, socializing, etc.).

How does a student-athlete fit all of these other activities into only 8 hours per day? Some athletes are unable to fit everything in, and their solution is to let their studies slide. It's the rare coach who will recognize that certain activities may be as important as (or even more important than) a player's athletics commitments. Many coaches recommend — or even demand — that their student-athletes take only 12 units during in-season terms (this is the least that a student can take and still be eligible for athletics). In addition, some coaches suggest that only easy courses, those that don't require 2 or 3 hours of study time per unit, be taken during the athlete's competitive season.

I used to go along with the idea that football players on scholarship were "student-athletes," which is what the NCAA calls them. Meaning a student first, an athlete second. We were kidding ourselves, trying to make it more palatable to the academicians. We don't have to say that and we shouldn't. At the level we play, the boy is really an athlete first and a student second.

Bear Bryant, University of Alabama's
legendary football coach [1]

In sports that have seasons that span the entire academic year, there is no off-season in which a student-athlete can take a heavier course load. A similar problem exists for athletes who must maintain year-round training schedules. Athletes in these circumstances who feel that they can handle only 12 or 13 units per term will probably have to take longer than four years to graduate. If your time commitment to athletics is 40 or more hours per week or if you are in an especially time-consuming major, you might seriously consider either attending summer sessions or stretching your college education over another term or year, rather than shortchanging either academics or athletics.

Sample Weekly Calendar

		Monday	Tuesday	Wednesday
Morning	6:00 AM	sleep	GIT/B	sleep
	7:00	GIT/B*	ANTHRO	GIT/B
	8:00	LAW	lib. read	LAW
	9:00	soc./nap	GOV'T	soc./nap
	10:00	study	study	study
	11:00	BIOL	soc./nap	BIOL
	12:00	BIO LAB	lunch	BIO LAB
Afternoon	1:00 PM	lunch	JOURN	eat/travel
	2:00	practice	practice	team travel
	3:00	practice	practice	travel/study
	4:00	practice	practice	travel/study
	5:00	prac/shwr	prac/shwr	travel/eat
Evening	6:00	dinner	dinner	gme prep
	7:00	Law group	write-J	game
	8:00	Law group	write-J	game
	9:00	Study Gov't	read-Bio	game
	10:00	study Gov't	read-Bio	gme/shwr
	11:00	read-Anth	sleep	read-Anth
	12:00	sleep	sleep	sleep
	1:00 AM	sleep	sleep	sleep

*GIT/B Get It Together/Breakfast

Thursday	Friday	Saturday	Sunday
GIT/B	sleep	sleep	sleep
ANTHRO	GIT/B	sleep	sleep
lib. read	LAW	GIT/B	GIT/B
GOV'T	soc./nap	laundry	chapel
weights	study	study	chapel
soc./nap	BIOL	lunch	study
lunch	lunch	bank, etc.	lunch
JOURN	study	gme prep	soc.
practice	practice	game	soc.
practice	practice	game	soc.
practice	practice	game	weights
prac/shwr	prac/shwr	game/shwr	dinner
dinner	dinner	rest	read Law
study	study	soc.	read Law
study	soc.	soc.	study
study	soc.	soc.	study
study	soc.	soc.	study
sleep	soc.	soc.	study
sleep	sleep	soc.	study
sleep	sleep	sleep	sleep

*GIT/B Get It Together/Breakfast

Weekly Calendar

		Monday	Tuesday	Wednesday
Morning	6:00 AM			
	7:00			
	8:00			
	9:00			
	10:00			
	11:00			
	12:00			
Afternoon	1:00 PM			
	2:00			
	3:00			
	4:00			
	5:00			
Evening	6:00			
	7:00			
	8:00			
	9:00			
	10:00			
	11:00			
	12:00			
	1:00 AM			

Thursday	Friday	Saturday	Sunday

You are a full-time student, a full-time athlete, and a full-time person. How will the three of you spend your 168 hours this week?

Organizing your study time. Since the time you have scheduled for studying is probably not the time you most look forward to, you'll have to take measures to make sure it is used efficiently. Doing the following will help to keep you from wasting your study time.

- Write down what you will begin the next study session with *before* the session begins. Identify the topic of your study session either in class or before you end the prior study session. This will help to get you out of the starting blocks quickly, the hardest part of studying.

- Just as most coaches lay out schedules detailing what will be covered that day, develop a plan for your study time. Make sure that each course is given adequate study time each week.

- When you use up the allotted time for one subject, leave it even if you aren't finished. Don't borrow from the next subject's study time. This will keep you from shortchanging a course and help you to be more efficient for the next study session.

- Daydreaming belongs to leisure time. Commit yourself to your study time and commit yourself to your play and leisure time. That way you'll enjoy and profit more from each activity.

- Avoid cramming for tests. Study a little at a time, but often. A set schedule helps you do this.

- Study for tests before going to sleep. Your subconscious mind tends to repeat the information while you sleep, in essence giving you more hours of study.

- If your mind wanders during a study session and you can't snap it back to the subject, take a 5-minute break (no longer), preferably alone. (Study breaks that involve other people tend to extend well beyond 5 minutes.) Some people need more short breaks than others, but everyone should be able to get through at least half an hour of study without a break.

- If your coach has set up study halls and you must (or want to) attend, sit toward the edge of the group where there is less chance of being disturbed.

- Keep a dictionary by your side as you study, and use it whenever you have the slightest doubt about the meaning of a word. When writing a paper, keep a dictionary, a thesaurus (for synonyms), and a manual of style close at hand, and refer to them regularly. Using these resources actually speeds up your studying and writing rather than slows you down, and you learn more each time rather than continuing to make the same mistakes.

One of the things that make smart people smart: they recognize what they *don't* know and look it up.

Improving the Learning Skills Needed for College-Level Work

Requirements for college graduation have been getting harder in recent years.[2] Colleges are asking more of their students because many graduates during the past ten or fifteen years simply haven't had the skills that college graduates should have. What are those skills?

Reading Competencies

- The ability to use a table of contents, preface, introduction, titles and subtitles, index, glossary, appendix, and bibliography.

- The ability to define unfamiliar words by using contextual clues and a dictionary.

Writing Competencies

- The ability to write standard English sentences with proper spelling, word choice, and grammar (including correct verb forms, punctuation, capitalization, pluralization, and possessive forms).
- The ability to improve one's writing by restructuring, correcting errors, and rewriting.

Speaking and Listening Competencies

- The ability to engage critically and constructively in an exchange of ideas, particularly during class discussions and conferences with instructors.
- The ability to answer and ask questions coherently and concisely, and to follow spoken instructions.

Mathematical Competencies

- The ability to use principles of algebra and geometry, including integers, fractions, and decimals; ratios, proportions, and percentages; and roots and powers.
- The ability to use elementary concepts of probability and statistics.

Reasoning Competencies

- The ability to recognize and use inductive and deductive reasoning, and to recognize fallacies in reasoning.
- The ability to distinguish between fact and opinion.

Studying Competencies

- The ability to set study goals and priorities consistent with stated course objectives, to establish surroundings and habits conducive to learning independently or with others, and to follow a schedule that accounts for both short- and long-term projects.
- The ability to locate and use resources external to the classroom (for example, libraries, computers, interviews, and direct observation), and to incorporate knowledge from such sources into the learning process.

Most colleges have facilities to help students improve reading, writing, speaking, listening, mathematics, reasoning, and general study skills. At such a learning skills center, or possibly through the academic advising or counseling centers, you can find assistance to help you improve areas in which you are weak. Colleges often hold workshops or minicourses that provide practical assistance in many of the following areas.

- Managing time and using it efficiently
- Developing memory skills
- Efficient listening and note-taking
- Preparing for and taking exams
- Getting more out of textbooks
- Understanding graphs and tables
- Improving reading efficiency
- Improving your vocabulary
- Solving math word problems
- Understanding and using basic statistics
- Working on fractions
- Using a calculator in schoolwork
- Using dictionaries and other reference books
- Efficient use of the school library

If your college offers programs in these areas, taking them is well worth the extra effort. They are often available free or for a modest fee. These workshops and minicourses are usually small (eight to fifteen students), so you will get much individual attention.

How to Handle Test Anxiety

Tests are a fact of college life. Few people enjoy taking them. Some people have the ability to relax during a test, but most of us feel at least a little nervous. Feeling anxious or nervous about a test comes from one or a combination of the following factors.

Fear of failure. The habit of feeling anxious when taking tests often begins with an early failure that has grown into an intense fear of failure. From that point, it becomes a self-fulfilling prophecy with the fear of failing causing failure to happen. You may have seen this happen to some athletes in competition. Athletes who are good in practice but not in contests often fail simply because they psych themselves out.

Lack of preparation. How you prepare for tests is something that is generally under your control. The answer to poor preparation as a source of anxiety, of course, is better preparation, which is what the previous sections of this chapter have been about.

Not liking to be compared with others. By the time they reach college, athletes generally have grown accustomed to being compared with others. However, some athletes may see the comparison of physical skills as very different from the comparison of knowledge or intellectual ability. Because they have internalized the dumb-jock image, they feel very confident and relaxed about physical comparisons but unsure and anxious about academic comparisons.

Belief that the outcome of the test is crucial to one's future success. Few tests in college are truly crucial to your future. You can usually counteract a poor grade on a particular test with good performance elsewhere in the class.

In sports events, athletes often thrive on mild spurts of anxiety. Nervousness gets the adrenalin flowing and they perform better than if they were "flat," that is, without some competitive anxiety. This is most obvious when facing a tough opponent, whom you know you must be up for in order to be competitive. As an athlete, you can take this healthful way of dealing with sports anxiety and apply it to test taking in school. Look upon tests as a challenge in which you "show those people what you can do." This attitude will motivate you to prepare well for the test and thus can help you benefit from moderate anxiety.

Courage is resistance to fear, mastery of fear—not absence of fear.

Mark Twain, *Puddin'head Wilson*

How to Respond to Poor Performance

Does a poor performance in your sport lead you to want to give it up or to slough off in practice and training because you now expect to do poorly? Not likely, or you wouldn't have come this far as an athlete. Instead, a poor performance probably makes you work harder toward the next challenge. There should be no difference between sports and schoolwork; in this respect, your brain works just as your body does. If you did poorly on a test or paper, the answer is probably *not* that you aren't smart enough. You simply need to devote more time to your work or direct your energies better. Instead of giving up, do what is necessary to improve—just as you would in your sport.

Also, check where you characteristically sit in class. It's much easier to stay alert and learn by sitting in the front and center of the classroom than in the back. Good students tend to select seats in a T-formation, with the crossbar formed by the first two rows. Students with poorer performance tend to sit in the back and to the sides. The attitude of those who sit near you in class is contagious, so it makes sense to sit with the good students.

As we stated earlier, whenever you are unsure of an instructor's meaning in what is said or written, ask for an explanation. Rarely is a question considered stupid, except in the mind of the person who asks it. And even if, in a moment of thoughtlessness, a professor or teaching assistant seems to put you down for your question or idea, everybody (with the possible exception of you) will forget about it in a matter of moments. Unless the professor indicates that he or she doesn't want questions and comments from the class, you'll find your courses to be more stimulating and a better learning experience if you take an active and confident part in them.

The Academic Pie

Your academic requirements — the number of credits you must earn and the courses you must take in order to graduate — may be thought of as ingredients in a pie that you have at least four years to consume. The pie is divided into three big slices, and all of the courses you take fit into one or another of those slices.

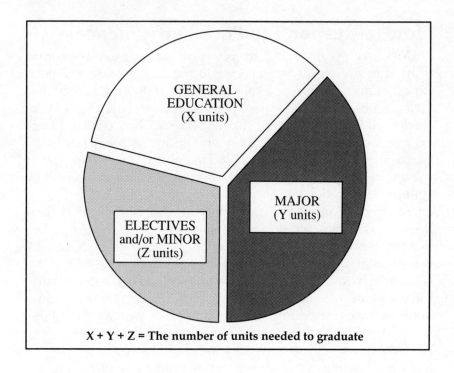

X + Y + Z = **The number of units needed to graduate**

General Education

General education, commonly called GE but also known on some campuses as distribution requirements, refers to a group of courses that all students must take, regardless of their majors. You'll begin taking these GE courses your first term in college, whether you go to a two-year or four-year institution.

The GE slice of the pie is intended to provide you with a well-rounded undergraduate education. It usually includes basic courses in English, history and government, natural sciences and mathematics, social sciences and humanities, possibly a foreign language, and courses designed for lifelong enjoyment, such as art appreciation and physical education. Some colleges require students to take courses in computer science.

GE is intended to broaden your interests and understanding rather than to address your career goals directly. Students who are particularly career oriented may resent having to "waste time" in GE courses since they can't see how GE will help them get a job. A well-rounded education *does* have career benefits, although they may not always be immediately apparent.

The exact pattern and number of units required in GE for graduation vary from one school to another. The GE areas and why they will benefit you are described below.

English and composition requirements. Communicating well isn't just knowing proper grammar and putting sentences together correctly. Good communication also means knowing how to develop thoughts, build an argument, and analyze and understand what other people say and write. Professors in most subject areas often reduce grades because of poor language skills. Take care of your English requirements as soon as possible. You are sure to benefit in your other classes as a result.

Writing is probably the single most important and useful life skill. If you dread writing, take courses that require it—just as all good athletes work on their weaknesses.

Think of your college-level English requirement this way: the more you dread it, the more you probably need it and the better it will be for you in the long run. Rather than view the English requirement as a hurdle, consider it an opportunity—maybe your last one—to get some help in developing your ability in the English language.

You may be one of the students who enter college with strong English skills. If your skills are strong enough, you may be exempt from the basic English requirement. But even if you are exempt, it's a good idea to take an intermediate or advanced composition course as an elective. Communication is as important as any skill you'll develop in college. It can always stand improvement.

History and government. The history and government courses all students must take are sometimes called the good-citizenship requirements. This suggests that if students know how their society has developed and how it works, they are more likely to support it as good citizens. Whether or not this is the case, all schools recognize that history and government contribute to an understanding of the social system in which we must function and so require a course or two in each. State-supported colleges often require students to take a course in state and local government.

Natural science and math. At least one term (often more) of a natural science is required of all undergraduates. Students can usually choose from biology, chemistry, physics, geology, geography, astronomy, and other natural or life sciences. Nonscience majors may be required to take a science course that includes a laboratory component in order to ensure that they have some hands-on experience with the scientific method of investigation and problem solving.

Some schools insist that a formal mathematics subject, such as algebra, trigonometry, or calculus, be used to fulfill the mathematics requirement. Others consider this requirement to be a way of improving your reasoning or computing skills and so allow students to fulfill the math requirement with courses in statistics or computer science. The purpose of this area of GE is to ensure that all students learn skills to help them make decisions through logical, systematic analyses.

Social science and humanities. Courses in sociology, psychology, anthropology, communication studies, ethnic and women's studies, law, economics, philosophy, and the arts are usually included in this area, as are the disciplines of history and political science. These subjects will help you understand the nature of social and cultural institutions and how people relate to one another as individuals and in small and large groups.

Foreign language. The foreign language requirement is making a comeback after years of disregard. Even beyond the obvious benefits of knowing another language (including increased employment marketability), studying another tongue can help you with your English skills. Many of us paid little attention to grammar when we learned English. But in order to learn another language as an adult, you have to understand its grammar, and in learning grammar you begin to understand your own language better. If you are faced with a foreign language requirement, you may feel like avoiding it for as long as possible (maybe hoping it will go away). Don't. Take it as early as possible in order to help improve your English skills.

Other GE requirements. This category includes those courses—physical education, dance, drama, art, and photography—designed to enrich the quality of your life through health and cultural activities. Any course credit coming to you from intercollegiate athletics will fall into this category, if it fits into GE at all.

Your Major

Whereas GE is designed to educate broadly in areas you might ordinarily avoid, a major—the second slice of your academic pie—lets you select a particular area of interest and allows you to dig deeply into it. Majors vary widely in the number of units required. Some liberal arts majors (such as psychology, history, or art) may require only about 30 units, while majors in applied or professional areas (such as engineering or nursing) require more. The exact unit requirements vary from school to school.

If you come to college undecided about a major field of study, use your general education courses and electives (discussed below) to poke around in various subject areas. A course in psychology, one in business, another in computer science, another in history, and one in English would give a student looking around for a major a very nice spread of subject areas from which to choose. During the next term, courses might be taken in social science, art or drama, government, math, and a natural science.

The criteria you should consider in selecting a major include (1) how much you enjoy the subject matter, (2) how well you are likely to perform in the field of study, (3) how well you think you will like the people in the department (students and faculty), and (4) how much the field of study will help you regarding future career goals. Some of these may be more important to you than others. In any case, you should pay attention to the first criterion because the more you enjoy your courses, the better your overall education will be.

Most students change majors during college. Is this bad? Not at all. Changing majors simply means your interests have changed, your first choice wasn't carefully considered, or you are finding out more about yourself. Changing majors may set back the time-table for getting your degree, but it's better than continuing in a major that no longer interests you.

Electives

The third slice of your academic pie includes the units you'll have to take beyond GE and major courses. These courses are sometimes called electives and can be used in a number of different ways. A minor might fit in nicely here, or even a second major, especially if both majors you are considering are light (require relatively few units). Another way to treat this third slice is to use it for those courses that you've always wanted to take but that don't fit into GE or your major. The only requirement for this third slice is that it be used to take enough units to give you at least the minimum number needed to graduate.

Some majors require a minor, which necessarily will cut into this third slice. For example, a criminal justice major who is specializing in forensic science might be required to take a chemistry minor. Or, a major in business administration with a specialization in international business might need a minor in a foreign language.

Your major may not require you to have an official minor but may still direct you to take several courses in a second area. For example, computer science majors often must take several courses in mathematics and statistics. In that situation, you might consider taking an additional course or two in this secondary area in order to earn an official minor, which would be noted as such on your transcript.

You may dip into many departments to find electives to satisfy your own educational interests or to help in career preparation. For example, if you contemplate a career in business, you may benefit from courses in psychology, political science, math, foreign languages, and even philosophy (an important background to have for problem solving). Many students find that taking a broad range of electives is the best strategy for developing career potential, because they can pick a combination of courses from several academic departments that will help most in a given field of work. This is called course clustering.

Don't feel that you have to aim for the minimum number of units required for graduation. Nothing (except, possibly, time and money) prevents you from taking more than that minimum. Taking extra units could turn out to be a wise and profitable decision in the long run, because you are using them to accumulate knowledge and skills that will help you in the future.

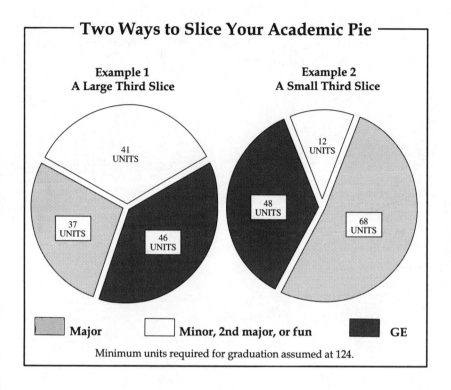

Two Ways to Slice Your Academic Pie

Example 1
A Large Third Slice

41 UNITS

37 UNITS

46 UNITS

Example 2
A Small Third Slice

12 UNITS

48 UNITS

68 UNITS

Major   Minor, 2nd major, or fun   GE

Minimum units required for graduation assumed at 124.

Other Graduation Requirements

Graduation requirements involve more than the number of units required in GE, your major, and electives. These other requirements include *a minimum number of upper-division units*, to ensure that you didn't take the easy way with a light major and a bagful of relatively unchallenging lower-level courses, and *a minimum number of units in residence*, to ensure that your degree bearing the school's name was derived largely from credits earned there. The residence requirement doesn't refer to where you live (on campus or off campus) but rather to your status of being enrolled and taking courses at that school. The residence requirement usually concerns only those who have transferred and spent less than two years at the school from which they intend to graduate, but students who have earned credits through more than one off-campus program may be affected as well.

This chapter has given you some ways to think about yourself as a student. It also explained some of the skills and requirements that are at the heart of a college education. This is not all you need to know about college, but it should provide a firm base from which you can make your way.

9

Athletics and Academics as Bridges to Career Success

The Role of Athletics in Career Preparation . . . Special Problems Facing Some Athletes . . . Athletics and College Is the Right Combination . . . How Your Education Is a Bridge to Career Success . . . Playing the Career Game with a Full Deck . . . A Word About Graduate School

What is most revealing about [Bill] Bradley is [that he] has made himself a great player; it wasn't a gift. . . . One of his roommates [at Princeton], . . . Coleman Hicks, says, "He isn't the smartest guy who ever woke up in the morning." But Bradley wound up winning a Rhodes [Scholarship] and Hicks says of him, "He's very special. He did more with what he had than anybody I know."

Tony Kornheiser, *Washington Post*[1]

Bill Bradley, former Princeton all-American, 1964 Olympics champion, Rhodes scholar, and NBA All Star for the New York Knicks, is now a highly respected U.S. senator from New Jersey. He grew up in a small town—Crystal City, Missouri. Bradley was intent upon getting the best education possible and used his education to transform his abilities into enormous accomplishments.

Sure, you say, an Ivy Leaguer! Anyone who comes from Princeton (or Harvard, or Yale, or Stanford, or . . .) can make it big! But it's not necessarily so. There are many Princeton failures, just as there are many successful politicians, executives, doctors, lawyers, scientists, and community leaders who graduated from all varieties of schools—ranging from large state universities to small colleges. Bradley made it as an athlete and a senator because of his personal qualities, not because of the school he attended. Many of the same qualities that Senator Bradley used to gain career success were ones that he nurtured in sports; they carried over to his pursuit of a career. The message to you? Because of your involvement in sports, you have a good shot at developing the qualities that can help lead to career success.

Are we telling you that sports in college are more than just games and contests, that sports relate to real life? Yes, without a doubt. We aren't just talking about help from fans who do favors for the players they once cheered. This may happen, but that kind of assistance is minor in terms of the contribution it can make to lasting career success. We are talking about how your experiences in athletics can make you more effective in a real job.

The element that will help you in your progress toward your career is the sports *experience,* not your stats and press clippings. All athletes, those who tend to win as well as those who tend to lose, can develop the qualities that spell career success. Because wins and losses are influenced by so many external forces—the level of competition, the fact that at least half of the competitors in sports have to lose in any contest (and all but one lose in the race for a championship), the quality of coaching, to name just a few— an athlete's strengths are often buried on a scorecard. A .220 hitter can become an executive as easily as a star hitter can, maybe even more easily, because the athlete with only average ability has had to work harder to achieve his or her level of success. What matters most is that as a college athlete you suited up every day, learned to prepare yourself for rigorous competition, took the good and the bad that came with competition, and kept going back for more.

Athletes are already one step ahead of many other college students in terms of career preparation, since they have worked, risked, succeeded, failed, recovered, and earned the self-respect that comes from doing their job—all while in the public eye. Your college sports career conditions you to perform under stress, to learn and adjust to variables rapidly, and to become self-disciplined, and it forces you to stretch to your full potential. This is what people must do to prepare for a career, and you've already practiced it in sports. The rigorous demands you've experienced in sports competition form an effective bridge to your future occupational challenges.

The profile of Alex Athlete on the following page is a summary of the thoughts that often go through a student-athlete's mind as that person begins thinking about a career and the skills we believe are desired in the job market. As you can see, participation in college sports can nurture many qualities that are valuable assets in any career.

The Role of Athletics in Career Preparation

How can college athletics help you to prepare for a career if you are not going to become a professional athlete? Many college athletes, and even many coaches, tend to view sports as separate from real-world employment. They have cast sports as play — however seriously they take them — and everything else as work. This separation is artificial, since diligent striving in any form is work, and a person's work capabilities, skills, and habits are affected by every activity in which he or she participates. Your participation in sports reveals a great many things about you, so pay attention to the messages you are already sending out to the world.

For the past few years, sports may have been your first priority, the area to which you have devoted much of your energy. In doing so, you have made a strong statement about your career potential. That statement is not about the *kind of work* that you expect to go into, but about the *kind of person* you are — highly motivated, hardworking, energetic, and willing and able to take instruction so that in due time you'll be capable of leading others. These qualities are highly valued by people who select employees and future organizational leaders, and that is where your athletics involvement enters the career picture. Athletics attract people who already possess strong personal qualities and provide an environment in which they can cultivate and expand these qualities. The intensity of intercollegiate competition is a particularly good crucible for testing the individual against his or her environment.

ALEX ATHLETE

EDUCATION: Good Ol' State University (or Friendlyville College)

GOAL: A career involving competition and teamwork, in which I can see the results of my efforts, develop new skills, and enjoy the whole experience while I'm doing it.

ALSO: Be around friends, have a few laughs, get some recognition for my work, and learn from smart people.

BUT: Who wants an ex-jock, anyway? All I know much about is sports—how to take orders from coaches, sweat, and keep my eye on the ball.

MEANWHILE: Careers are stocked with college graduates who are goal directed and can translate their drives into action and performance.

CONCLUSION: What chance do I have to reach my goal?

SKILLS GAINED AS AN ATHLETE:
    Physical and mental alertness
    Endurance and persistence
    Ability to concentrate on goals/objectives
    Ability to work well with others
    Loyalty, supportive of group goals
    Ability to deal well with setbacks or defeats
    Ability to organize time well

WORK SITUATIONS WHERE AN ATHLETE'S SKILLS ARE NEEDED:
    Large corporations
    Small businesses
    Educational organizations
    Public agencies/federal government
    Performing arts/communication organizations
    Nonprofit organizations
    Family businesses
    Self-employment
    et cetera

REVISED CONCLUSION:
    I can work anywhere. An athlete has qualities suitable for every sort of career. I must recognize these qualities in myself before anyone else will.

In a rapidly developing field such as telecommunications, we need college graduates who have developed skills both in the classroom and on the playing field. Every technical project at AT&T Bell Laboratories involves teamwork as well as technical expertise.

Gale Hiering Varma, recruitment
manager, AT&T Bell Laboratories

Employers look for the job candidate who can be trained, is receptive to learning, strives for perfection, follows organization goals, looks for new challenges, and supports other people in the organization. All coaches want these qualities in their players. If you are the kind of athlete who pushes toward your personal limits, you have a four-year head start on the development of work habits and the highly motivated attitudes that employers most desire.

All this is great in theory, you might be thinking, but what can you do right now, while still in college, to help your chances of a successful career? The following guidelines will show you specifically how to use sports as a bridge to career success.

Cultivate the abilities, behaviors, and attitudes toward work demanded in your sport that translate into competence in any kind of job. Improve your interaction with teammates and coaches; self-discipline, risk-taking, and creative strategies (e.g., developing alternative plans); and management of time. To people who run organizations, it is self-evident that success in athletics develops leadership qualities, primarily because the attributes that contribute to a winning team are often needed to keep members of a company or agency pulling together.

Build up the mental component of your sport. A good level of physical fitness will help somewhat in your future work, but the mental qualities that you bring to it will be far more crucial. The toughness you need to endure grueling practices, overcome pain and injuries, and accept losses in order to bounce back with a better performance in the future breeds personal qualities that you can use in your career. Emotional endurance and resilience are as necessary for an executive or a scientist as they are for a trained athlete. The mental side of your athletics also cultivates a spirit of reasonable risk-taking and a willingness to accept the consequences of your actions. The emotional steadiness of an athlete who stands up to crises and enjoys pressure is highly valued in the world of work.

Get involved in pregame strategic planning. Get as close as you can to the thinking that produces results on the field. Involve yourself in the mental preparation that precedes a game, either by working with the coaches or by studying the books and manuals of your sport. Participate in strategy talks when and where you can. Make a habit of asking "Why?" Even sports such as tennis, swimming, gymnastics, and track and field, in which competition is one-on-one, strategies such as pacing, psychological combat with opponents, and the judicious placement of individuals in particular events are involved.

No matter what sport you are in, don't just leave the thinking up to coaches and captains. If they don't want to hear your opinion, listen to what they are thinking and why. Use your sport to train your mind, weigh alternatives, and plan and adjust; this is the way a college graduate seeking success in a career will be *expected* to think.

Find opportunities to teach your sport to others. Teach children, sports-minded folks, high school athletes, and others your sport. (Remember, however, that you cannot be paid for this, other than expenses, if you want to keep your eligibility.) Teaching helps to build communication skills — talking, explaining the way you see things, listening and trying to understand the way others see things — as well as a general sensitivity to other people. Most jobs involve teaching in one form or another, so the earlier you learn to communicate your ideas and perspectives to others, the better. Teaching can also be a form of salesmanship, in that you try to get others hooked on your viewpoint, or persuade them to appreciate different views. "Here's how I see it . . ." operates in all forms of work.

Mingle with nonathletes as much as you can. To get a broader perspective on what life after college will be like, get acquainted with people whose interests and abilities differ from yours. Athletics can be a very closed, insulated world. Limiting yourself to jock talk can lead you to believe there's nothing else going on. Talk with students who don't care about athletics; get into town and meet community people, especially those who don't know that you are an athlete. Talk about what *they* do, not what you do. If your life in college has been wrapped up in sports and classes, take up an activity that has nothing to do with athletics — something that forces you to reach people whose interests are entirely different from yours. Broaden your perspective beyond your circle of athletics friends through elective courses as well as through the places you go and the people you choose to hang around with.

Make use of your public recognition. Most athletes are not known publicly by name and reputation, but their school and sport are likely to be. Take advantage of the relatively public nature of athletics. During team trips, try to meet people in work situations that interest you and get some exposure to their places of work, if possible. Every out-of-town contact expands your frame of reference for making a career choice.

It is, of course, especially useful to open dialogue with someone who might have either a job available or inside information on a particular career area. Naturally, you wouldn't go up to this person and just say: "Hi! My name is Josie and I played basketball at Ol' U. How's about a job?" But the following approach, or something like it, could get the ball rolling.

> "Pleased to meet you, Mr. Smith. I've been wanting to talk to someone like you who knows a lot about ___. Playing basketball at Ol' U. and keeping up with my schoolwork take up so much time that I haven't had much chance to explore what life is really like in your field."

At this point, Mr. Smith may pick up your lead and talk about sports or life as an athlete. If so, great! This should completely melt the ice and allow you to slide easily into career talk. But even if Mr. Smith doesn't want to talk sports, it gives him an image of you as a striving, hardworking, interesting person.

Don't be afraid to promote yourself. As an athlete, you may have had press interviews or at least conversations with friends in which you projected an "Aw, shucks" modesty about your accomplishments. Modesty does little good when you are trying to advance your career interests. Tell people that you believe you possess the potential for success in your career. Other college graduates have career aspirations similar to yours, and interviewers will pay the most attention to those who show the greatest drive and self-confidence.

Many people interpret modesty as lack of self-confidence. While you may not intend that your modesty be interpreted that way, how others see you is important in career concerns. So, put aside your modesty and say in a straightforward way what you have done and can do. Don't go overboard; there is a clear line between bragging and an honest accounting of yourself.

The Unique Career Value of Being an Athlete

If you take full advantage of your experience as an athlete, you will develop several qualities and abilities that are highly valued by employers.

1. **Endurance and persistence:** The ability to persevere in working toward objectives—to last through slow times and uncertain progress—is a plus in any endeavor. Sheer endurance in the face of fatigue is a virtue and often leads to good results.

2. **Physical and mental alertness:** Every employer wants people who can put all their energy toward the tasks at hand. Athletes are accustomed to being physically and mentally fit. They are unlikely to be dragged down by illnesses or laziness.

3. **Goal directedness:** The athlete's ability to organize himself or herself toward a goal and keep working doggedly toward that goal is highly prized by the business world and other employers. Athletes have the capacity to persist in working toward specific, measurable achievements.

4. **Ability to work well with others:** Otherwise known as being a team player, this quality is well understood by athletes, as they have learned to cooperate with teammates under the most intense and demanding conditions.

5. **Loyalty:** Every athlete understands and appreciates the importance of making personal needs second to the goals of the group. Today loyalty seems to be in short supply, but athletes continue to respect this quality and bring it to the

workplace (it's another attribute highly regarded by employers).

6. **Resilience:** No activity in life is more certain to have defeats than sports. Athletes learn to handle the emotions involved in losing and to develop the ability to come back in the next round with renewed enthusiasm. This quality comes in handy when other workers are complaining about setbacks and allowing themselves to be slowed down.

7. **Ability to organize time well:** Given that student-athletes have two jobs in one, they learn how to manage their time under the most demanding conditions. This quality transfers well to work situations, where there are always more tasks to be done than time available to do them.

Special Problems Facing Some Athletes

Although it may be comforting to know that athletes have unique advantages that carry beyond their playing field experience, you may be facing a particular problem as a student-athlete, something that is not shared by athletes in general but is a definite source of trouble for you. The athletics experience affects people in different ways. While many athletes benefit from their competitive experience, many others suffer — for example, from the "ghetto"-izing effect of athletics (when they associate only with other athletes). Some athletes have a hard time accepting themselves as candidates for the real world. Note the special problems of the athletes in the following brief profiles and ways that they could overcome them.

I felt my whole life had revolved around basketball. I didn't apply my intelligence [while in college] because basketball was all I cared about. I thought I'd be successful at anything, just because I enjoyed success at basketball. But I was wrong, and it took me two or three years to readjust and get into the real world.

A former college athlete [2]

137

Fast-Bucks Freddie: I see so much money being made in sports that it seems stupid to consider doing anything else as a career. Why should I work for a living when I can play? If I don't make it as a player, maybe I can organize sports events — anything to stay close to where the money is.

Answer to Fast-Bucks: There's a little Fast-Bucks in all of us. This is not so much a personal deficiency, Freddie, as it is your desire to get on the gravy train. You simply are unwilling to believe that anything else might compete with what you see as your golden opportunity.

You're right about the riches that await a few people who mine the sports world. But it takes more luck than talent to be one of those rare people. You have to allow for the facts of life in sports: franchises die, whole sports leagues die, players get injured, strikes occur, and darned few people earn an income in sports for more than a handful of years. The professional-sports graveyard is littered with sure things — women's professional basketball and softball, professional track and field, team tennis, and professional coed volleyball, to name a few.

If you still want to give it a try after understanding all this, in the immortal words of Rocky Balboa, "Go for it!" Nothing is sacred about working 9 to 5 in a regular job. Try your luck and don't second-guess yourself. But be prepared to accept the likelihood that you'll have a hard time making any money, let alone fast bucks. Nobody makes easy money. Scratch someone who seems to be an overnight success, and you'll probably find a person who suffered many failures along the way.

Never-Made-It Norbert: For every name in the newspapers, there are 1,000 of me. Even when I don't get cut from the squad, I never see much action. I have to explain to friends why my uniform never gets dirty and why I'm on campus when the team is traveling. I train hard, try hard, have some ability, and eat the right foods but never get beyond the sidelines. My feeling of failure is causing me to have doubts about my job and career prospects. Are my failures in sports trying to tell me something? Is a loser a loser in everything?

Answer to Norbert: If being a success in college sports were a reliable indicator of future achievement, the top corporations would hire only varsity lineups, and most politicians would be ex-jocks. Neither, however, is true. You'll find varsity heroes in the gutter, and third-stringers in boardrooms. The marketable qualities that athletics breed are available to *all* members of the team, not just those in the starting lineup. For all who compete with dedication, willingness to learn, and enthusiasm, the primary effect of collegiate sports is to produce qualities that are valued in the work world. You obviously have dedication and persistence, and these traits will show in your favor when you are involved in a career where people are not seen as either winners or losers but rather as good or bad workers and leaders. All members of a working team can win, and unlike sports, where only one team or person can be champ, many organizations in the same field come out winners.

Footloose Frieda: Competing in sports is such a roller coaster ride, I don't ever want to get off. Even if I won't ever be a millionaire, I want to live like one — taking trips, being taken care of, seeing important people, and having them care about what I do — just as it has been in college sports. Athletics can provide such a millionaire life-style and pace that anything else seems as dull as dishwater by comparison. The idea of a 9-to-5 existence makes me sick. I know I'm jaded about the real world and unrealistic about the sports world, but I love it.

Answer to Frieda: We're as much in favor of an exciting life as anyone. Boredom is the worst curse of the working world. However, realize that your present high life-style has been supported by your college, which believes that your success on the field in some way has something to do with higher learning. That party will eventually end. That doesn't mean the fun will end, only that the game changes. Be ready for the change, and roll with it—if you want to continue enjoying life. Before the collegiate party ends, work on developing talents that someone in the work world wants. The more talents you have to offer, the farther you will go in a career and the more fun and excitement you will have.

Athletics and College Is the Right Combination

In the dual life you lead as a student-athlete, it's not your association with the sport that is marketable but rather the obstacles you've overcome to keep competing in your sport while prospering as a student. Being able to do both things well sets you on the path to your future success. It is your bridge from college to career.

Athletics have as much carryover to other careers as anything else you might have done outside the classroom—probably more. However, if you allow athletics to isolate you from the mainstream of thought and experience in college and make you feel like an alien in areas that don't involve athletics, you have yourself to blame. You will have allowed yourself to be defeated by the very thing—your athletics experience—that could have made you special and particularly attractive to potential employers.

Right now you are surrounded by one of the most intelligent, creative, and socially concerned groups of individuals—a campus community—that you may ever be close to. You have easier access to the members of this community than you ever will have to any similar group of people. Take full advantage of the intellectual and creative stimulation they provide and their interests and knowledge. Make yourself more than just an athlete, and let both college and your experiences in sports lead you to success beyond college.

Persistence and Thoroughness Pay Off

Mike Cotten always looked more like a guard than a quarterback, but in 1961 he got his chance for stardom. The starting quarterback for the University of Texas at Austin was hurt at the beginning of that season, and Mike was thrust into the leadership role. He led the team to a winning season, a national ranking, and a victory in the Cotton Bowl over Ole Miss.

In spite of such brilliant successes in his sport, Cotten had his sights set on a career outside of sports from the start. He comments, "I knew early on that I did not have the physical attributes to make it as a professional. So I made sure that I was going to get my degree."

Cotten completed a law degree at the University of Texas Law School and today is a successful attorney in an Austin law firm. He attributes his achievements in both athletics and career more to persistence and thoroughness than to innate talent: "In football, I was short, not especially fast, and others had more talent. However, persistence and thoroughness of preparation for each game paid off for me. It has been the same way in my law work. Others are more intellectual, but I have done well because I take care to attend to everything that needs to be done in preparing for a trial."

Cotten believes strongly that the intensity of competition in collegiate sports gives any athlete an advantage in the career he or she pursues. "If you look for it, you can find competition in just about anything you can do," he asserts. "Any situation in which you are challenged either mentally or physically will bring out the best in you."

How Your Education Is a Bridge to Career Success

All the things you do off the field are important for your career development; academic and out-of-class activities enable you to gain the skills, knowledge, and experiences that employers want. Since you can't depend upon athletics alone to lead to a future career, you must examine how nonathletic accomplishments can build your career potential. Some student-athletes waste their time when practice sessions are over, while others are building a wide array of talents. What follows are ways to help you get the maximum benefit out of all your classroom obligations and choose out-of-class activities wisely.

The "Career = Major" Myth

Chances are that sometime soon you'll find yourself engaged in the following conversation (if you haven't already).

> "So, you're a student at _____ College. What are you studying there?"
> "Well, my major is _____."
> "That sounds like a good field to go into."

This frequently occurring exchange seems innocent enough, but it points out one of the great misunderstandings about how college education relates to career. Many people see a college education simply as vocational training: you choose a major, study it, graduate, and then go into the real world and perform what you've been trained to do. It seems so clean and simple, and, while they are attending classes, writing papers, and taking exams, students get some comfort from thinking that at a designated time they will be able to get a job and earn a living by using what they're learning. But this comfortable connection between major and career does not, in most cases, match the real world of work.

Majors are artificial and convenient constructions contrived by the academic world. The real reason that courses of study are organized into majors is to provide a focus for the departments in a college; majors provide common ground for the work of faculty members in each department. Majors are *not* created by colleges in cooperation with the labor market. Sometimes the field you study may correspond to available jobs, but often it is difficult to make the transition between an area of study, for instance, biology or chemistry, and the fields of work you might apply it to, in that case perhaps product development in industry. Or you may study a field—classics, mythology, or comparative literature— that has no apparent relationship at all to the workaday world. In another common scenario, students take a particular major expecting to get a job in an associated field, such as teaching or civil engineering, only to find that the job boom that had attracted them to the field in the first place peaked and passed in the four or five years it took them to get the degree.

Clinging to your major as if it were a guarantee to future success is both shortsighted and self-defeating. Keeping the career=major myth afloat may lead you to believe falsely that the courses you take are sufficient currency to buy you a job. Students who rely on course credits to carry them to a job are like athletes who depend solely on natural talent to succeed. Just as athletic success comes from a combination of natural talent, coaching, training, teamwork, and mental preparation, so does career success result from much more than the courses that appear on your transcript. You can use your major as far as it will take you, but you must be ready and able to draw on other resources when the major does not close the sale.

Playing the Career Game with a Full Deck

What are the resources available to you in college, and how can they help you prepare for a career? The remainder of this chapter describes a deck of cards from which you may choose as many cards as you like. Each has potential value for you in a job or career. The more individual cards you hold in your hand, the better you'll be able to play the career game.

As with a real deck of playing cards, the college-to-career deck has four suits. They are Knowledge, Generic Skills, Experience, and Personal Contacts.

The Knowledge Suit

Vocational and career training in college tend to be concentrated in those fields where the technical knowledge component is high. Many fields cannot be studied by focusing primarily on specialized knowledge. Business administration, journalism, politics, and many other areas of study are concerned less with specific bits of procedural knowledge and more with transmitting general conceptual knowledge and understanding. For this reason, a specific major is generally *not* a requirement for employment in such fields. People who have not majored in these areas have proved to be just as successful in these jobs as people who have completed the associated majors.

Put another way, the cards in the Knowledge suit will have high value in technical fields, such as engineering or computer science. The Knowledge cards you hold will always have some value, but just how valuable they will be to your career is difficult to assess in less technical fields.

Judy chose an education major, with science as her subject-area focus, because it seemed practical to have a teaching certificate. But she didn't really like teaching — she liked tennis far better and played on the team for four years. She frequently wondered what she would do with herself after graduation. Judy had taken a wide variety of communication skills courses because she liked them and had worked one summer for a book publisher, where she developed several contacts. Judy also had started a newsletter for her national sorority. She used all of these experiences to find work as an assistant editor for a popular science magazine after graduation. Although Judy did find her major concentration to be instrumental in securing her job, other aspects of her college experience and extracurricular activities far outweighed her major in leading Judy into a satisfying career. What's more, the things she learned in her major courses have served Judy well in her publishing job in very different ways from those she had expected as a student.

Focusing too much attention on selecting the right major (i.e., the one that will guarantee career success) is like asking: "Should I practice fielding grounders so I can be the best second baseman, or should I work on hitting homers so I can bat cleanup, or should I practice stealing bases so I can be the best base runner?" One-dimensional people are of limited use. To prepare for your sport, you work to become the most complete performer you possibly can. To be a successful career seeker — and to gain more cards in the Knowledge suit — try to get maximum knowledge from *all* your courses.

The Generic Skills Suit

If jobs could talk, they would say that all this fretting over what is the right major is putting your emphasis on the wrong suit. While some jobs do correlate directly with specific college majors, a far larger portion do not. *The most important fact of life in the job market is that most careers are learned and developed on the job, not prepared for in school.*

Generic skills are far more important than particular courses of study, in terms of both the breadth of jobs they prepare you to perform and the long-range growth and advancement potential they give you in whatever field you enter. Generic skills come in many forms — writing, speaking, research, computer use, problem solving, imagining, detail work, and so on. But, once again, if jobs could talk, they would emphasize strongly that skills are most useful when acquired *in combination.* That is, those who succeed, especially in leadership positions, do so because of their having many different skills, as many cards in the Generic Skills suit as they can acquire. There are more similarities among the people at the top than there are differences. And these similarities tend to be centered in the area of generic skills.

You studied finance and accounting and management science. You learned about economics, organizational behavior, and strategic planning. And you did all of this on the premise that this knowledge, that these tools you now possess, would carry you into your business careers, and give you the base to do the jobs you hoped you'd be hired to do.

Well, ladies and gentlemen, I'm here today to tell you that it may not be sufficient. We already have a lot of people in business today who can analyze financial statements. But what we need are more people of integrity and vision. We need people with intuition and good judgment, with sound values and the capacity to truly think.

Samuel H. Armacost, president,
BankAmerica Corporation [3]

The individual cards in the Generic Skills suit are as follows:

Technical skills. Regardless of the career you hope to enter, you should have some technical literacy. This means enough exposure to technical courses that you have an understanding of new developments in science and technology, especially computer technology.

Mathematical skills. Many colleges allow students to skip or minimize their face-to-face contact with mathematics, but you'll be painting yourself into a corner careerwise if you allow yourself to do this. Business is mathematical, as are public policy and many other areas, if you look closely enough—even music, for instance. Mathematical thinking is used to solve business problems, design interiors, plan research studies, and work on many social issues. In short, quantitative problems are everywhere, and you should learn to think in those terms.

If you are still cringing from this suggestion because you have a hard time understanding and appreciating the Xs and Ys of math, consider taking a statistics course in the departments of mathematics, sociology, psychology, education, or economics.

Writing skills. Writing skills are learned not only in writing courses, but they are also developed in courses that do not have "writing" or "composition" in the title. Any course that requires you to write reports or term projects or even to take essay exams can help to develop your writing skills.

Every challenging job that carries responsibility requires writing skill in some form. Clear, concise writing is the clearest sign of an intelligent, well-educated individual. You can be sure that prospective employers will examine your writing ability in the letters you send, on your application form, and in other situations.

Speaking skills. Courses to enhance your speaking skills are difficult to find in a college curriculum. Beyond public speaking courses (very useful for anyone at any stage in college), the courses that push you to become a better speaker tend to have small classes in which professors are more inclined to ask for oral reports and in-class reactions to lectures or readings and to have classroom debates. Speaking skills can also be cultivated outside the classroom in student government positions as well as on the debating team.

People who cannot express ideas orally to others are severely limited in their career development. If you don't like speaking in class or anywhere else in public, now is the time to develop this skill, not later. If you make mistakes while learning to speak in public in college, you might be embarrassed, but it will pass.

Research skills. The skill of assembling information relevant to a problem is useful in many careers. This skill can be developed in science courses, history courses, and any course in which you must gather information from primary or secondary sources.

Analytical/problem-solving skills. Problem solving is the most widely applied and universal skill of all, as it encompasses the ability to think logically. Science courses seem to be the most obvious for nurturing this skill, but many other courses emphasize it as well, including philosophy, critical thinking, and many liberal arts courses. Any course in which students are given a chance to identify and analyze problems and find solutions will provide an opportunity to develop these skills.

The entire hidden curriculum of generic skills should form a very basic part of your college education. Scientists must write and talk to others, managers must comprehend math and science, physical educators and recreation leaders must analyze and communicate, communicators must solve problems, and even social-service workers must understand computers. A skill is powerful not by itself but rather in combination with other skills. Focusing your efforts on mastering one or a few skills to the exclusion of others may make your college learning experience easier, but it will be at the expense of your career potential. You might as well learn to be a superb dribbler on the basketball court and ignore shooting, defense, and moving without the ball. As a designated dribbler, your use to any organization you join is limited and minor. If someone is to be eliminated from the organization, it will be the one with limited skills. The boss will be looking for someone who can do it all.

College graduates who are deficient in their writing, mathematical, scientific, or speaking skills tend to become worse later on, rather than better, because they have learned to avoid and fear these skill areas. The longer you wait to enhance a particular skill, the less likely it is that you will ever do it—certainly not once you are on the job.

The Experience Suit

Together with relevant academic knowledge from course work and a variety of generic skills, the Experience suit can give you a strong hand in the job market. But here is where the age-old lament of recent college graduates hunting for jobs is so often heard: "They're hiring only experienced people, and no one will give me the experience!" How do you build your Experience suit while still in school—*before* you have to lay the cards down to be evaluated by prospective employers? How can you get relevant work experience while you are trying to be both a full-time student and a full-time athlete?

Most colleges offer the following forms of career-relevant experiences.

Internships. Sometimes called a field experience, an internship gives you the opportunity to relate your academic background to a work situation. (In the medical and teaching professions, internships are requirements for a degree.) You may, for example, work in a child guidance clinic in order to apply your course work in adolescent psychology or social work. Or, as a student interested in earth sciences, you may work with an environmental agency collecting data about water pollution, erosion, and chemical interactions in local streams. In some internships, you can receive pay and/or academic credit. Since internships are gobbled up quickly, look for them early and ask how to integrate them into your course program.

Cooperative education programs. A co-op is usually a paid work experience, arranged by your college with a participating employer. Alternating programs schedule a semester of study followed by a semester of work. Concurrent or parallel programs schedule study and work in the same semester.

Independent study or research. An academic department often allows its students to do a special project or study that is not connected to a particular course. A student interested in advertising, for example, might do an independent study of the TV commercials that people in a geographic area recall seeing during the previous night's viewing. The student who conducts such research benefits in several ways: he or she (1) earns academic credit, (2) gains good personal contacts with the project adviser and TV station managers, (3) shows prospective employers that he or she has initiative and experience in advertising-related work, and (4) acquires useful knowledge in an area of primary concern to people who hire young advertising talent. Independent study or research allows you to observe a career area and gain knowledge about it as it exists in the real world at the same time you are studying it for academic purposes.

Practical courses. Many courses listed in the catalog offer students an opportunity to gain experience in a work setting or to perform functions that are regarded as practical experience in the workaday world. These include scientific laboratory courses, studio or applied arts courses, and courses emphasizing field studies, including anthropology, geology, health administration, forestry, and many others. Those who major in a given department may receive preference for enrolling in these courses, but don't assume that having a specific major is required. Frequently, such courses are open to nonmajors, presuming that they satisfy the prerequisites.

Many things you do in college for which you receive no course credit can also serve as cards in your Experience suit. Among these are jobs, volunteer work, and campus activities.

Jobs. It's nice to earn as much money as you can, but if you have the chance to work in a field that provides experience for a future profession—even if for low pay—it may be worth more in the long run to take it. Many part-time, summer, or campus jobs offer the chance to work with professionals in a field you hope to enter.

Volunteer work. Often, students are unable to land a paying job that offers relevant career experience, but they can get that experience by working as a volunteer. It you find yourself in this situation, the understanding between you and the employer should be that you are there for a learning experience: you provide your time and energy in exchange for what you can learn about the field while on the job. Such experience is likely to make a difference when you apply for a full-time job after graduation.

Campus activities. Your involvement in campus activities provides certain skills and experience that can be translated into relevant background for a future job. From treasurer of the Varsity Club to house manager of a fraternity or sorority to spokesperson for a dormitory, these kinds of experiences enable you to build generic skills and show evidence of taking responsibility, something employers like to see. Such involvements may seem like dead time, as they cut into your own time for leisure pursuits, but organizational work in college translates nicely to the organizational teamwork that all employers want their workers to manifest. Participating in campus activities tells employers that you are building people skills and are project oriented. This puts you ahead of the job applicant who has only taken courses and played sports. College students who do not have such experiences are often perceived as loners, overly book oriented, or perhaps not interested in other people. Much of the business of the world takes place in social groups; thus your experience in groups makes you more attractive as a potential employee.

The Personal Contacts Suit

Contacts are available to any student-athlete who makes the effort to find and talk with them. They can be your neighbors at home, relatives, parents of friends, professors, alumni — in fact, anyone you meet. For you as an athlete, potential contacts are numerous because you travel frequently, meet new people, and generally have more exposure to the public than most students.

Keep your career-antenna raised and active. Get in the habit of asking those whom you meet: "What work do you do?" If the answer seems interesting to you, ask, "May I talk with you some-time about it?" or, "What advice can you give me about preparing for work in _____, and whom should I talk with about getting a job?" Contacts should be approached as sources of information and potential links to employment.

Many of your easiest initial contacts are available right on campus. Faculty, coaches, and friends all may know people who work in fields that interest you. The act of establishing contacts tends to lead you to more contacts, and you can't have too many cards in your Personal Contacts suit. The first few contacts you make begin a networking process that looks much like the branching of a tree. The more contacts you make, the more you will know about a field of work. And the more people who know you are interested in a particular field, the more likely it is that some of them may either know of a job or have a job available when you are ready. A full discussion of making and using contacts is presented in Chapter 11.

Use All the Cards in Your Hand

The more cards you accumulate in each of the four suits — Knowledge, Generic Skills, Experience, and Personal Contacts — the greater the number of choices and the better career alternatives you will have. The best time to gather these cards is while you are an undergraduate. Paying attention to your hand will give you a sense of direction as well as strategies for further exploration. Even if you are not yet ready to pick a career direction, gather your cards and build strength in the suits. They will pay off regardless of your major or the career choices that you eventually make.

A Word About Graduate School

There is a continuing movement toward professionalization of certain fields of work, which often means that a master's or even a doctoral degree may be required for entry into the job market in those fields. Often, a particular undergraduate program (either a major or a specified combination of courses) is required for admission to a graduate degree program, but don't assume that this is always the case — find out firsthand from the graduate school that you'd like to attend what it requires. Sciences represent one extreme (a science major or many specific science courses are usually required for entry to graduate science programs), while law school represents the opposite extreme (no particular undergraduate program is required for admission). Although many people assume that a master's degree in business (an M.B.A.) requires an undergraduate business major, this is seldom the case. Liberal arts majors and others are equally welcome in most M.B.A. programs, though some schools may insist upon a certain number of math or economics courses.

Admission to graduate school generally depends upon the courses you take as an undergraduate, the grades you earn, and your ability to score well on graduate school admissions tests. Graduate and professional schools vary so widely in terms of how these requirements might be combined (two schools offering the same graduate program will differ) that you must inquire directly of each school that interests you. Your safest assumption is that each school will have different entrance requirements.

A growing trend in certain professional graduate programs — graduate business schools being one of them — is that applicants who have had some full-time work experience in the field have a better chance of being admitted. They are regarded as more highly motivated, more mature and committed to a career in that area, and more knowledgeable about the field. This trend is far from universal, however, and thousands of recent bachelor's degree graduates are admitted directly into professional schools each year.

Graduate school may seem like a long way off, and you may prefer to work for a while before applying to an advanced degree program. But if you really want to work in a profession in which an advanced degree is required (or in one that gives advanced-degree holders a clear advantage over other job applicants), you should begin preparing for graduate school as early as your junior year. Check with advisers and graduate school catalogs to see what skills are required (statistics? a foreign language? familiarity with computers?) and what particular undergraduate courses are prerequisite to the graduate programs that interest you.

10

Careers in and out of Sports

Looking into Athletics-Related Careers . . .
A Roster of Career Possibilities . . .
Careers Outside of Sports

The best game plan in choosing a career is to have a Plan A (the plan you will try first) and a Plan B (the one you will turn to if the first plan doesn't work out). For many college athletes, Plan A is likely to be a career relating to sports, and Plan B will be an alternative to sports. In this chapter, we urge you to consider both plans and recognize that the two may be related to each other. The sports-related jobs you may be considering are generally part of larger fields of endeavor. For example, coaching is part of the larger sphere of education, sportswriting is part of the larger spheres of journalism and all the communications media, and sports-related businesses suggest private enterprise in general.

Looking into Athletics-Related Careers

Taking a Shot at the Olympics or the Pros

Let's say your Plan A is to take a shot at becoming an Olympic athlete or to see if you can earn a living in professional sports. You already know that the odds weigh heavily against you. To give yourself this chance, you may be investing a lot of money in training and travel or borrowing money that you don't have. More likely than not, friends, family, and others are giving you the mixed message of "Go for it!" and "Get serious; prepare for a real career."

> *A lot of people leave school, put their eggs in one basket and then don't make it. They have no education, and it's tragic. . . . It's a short life on the circuit. Your body is so vulnerable. It's only a question of time before something breaks down. That's why you always have to be prepared.*
>
> Ferdi Taygan, professional tennis player [1]

Long odds aside, we still like to see people have the experience of shooting for the stars. You can aim for your lofty goal *and* keep an eye toward the career you might enter later. Here are several precautions we recommend to those in pursuit of a professional sports career.

- Minimize your financial risk by encouraging a company or organization to sponsor you. (If you are in a team sport and are drafted immediately, you may not need to take this step.) If you are trying to make it as a golfer or tennis player or as a free agent in a team sport, finding a sponsor may allow you to commit the extra time, energy, and concentration that might make the difference. Ask someone, or several people, to invest in your athletic future; in return, you will have to agree to share a percentage of your earnings with the sponsors, in the event you make it to the pros. Some words of caution: never make an open-ended deal. Place limits on how much your sponsors will invest and on either how much they can earn or for how many years the deal will last. In any event, be fully aware of the financial risks you face in your quest for a career in sports. Never put yourself in so great a financial bind that you hurt your chances for developing career alternatives in the future.

- If you haven't already graduated, complete your college degree as soon as possible. It's virtually certain that the kind of employment you will aspire to after being a professional athlete will require a degree. The number of jobs in every field of work for which a college degree is required or preferred is increasing. Getting a degree is the best insurance you have against future career difficulties. In this way, you will avoid going straight to the bottom in earning power after your pro career ends.

- If possible, obtain off-season or part-time jobs, preferably in areas that provide experience that can be marketed after your professional sports career ends. This means taking a job that holds some prospect for career development rather than taking any old job to fill time between seasons and earn pocket money.

- Develop an "If I were injured tomorrow" scenario, so that you have a strategy you can use if your career in sports should end suddenly. By having a contingency plan, you won't have the added burden of wondering "What will I do if . . . ?" while you are still competing. If you deal with this looming question at the proper time — before the crisis occurs — and free from pressure, this kind of negative thinking (what to do in case something bad happens) can help you to survive through rough times.

Are There Special Careers for Ex-athletes?

As a student-athlete, have you imagined or hoped that you would stay in sports in some way, even when your playing days end? Have you considered being a coach, scout, radio announcer, sportswriter, or players' agent? There are three major categories of nonplaying athletics-related careers.

1. Careers in which previous experience as a player is almost always essential, such as coaching and scouting.

2. Careers in which experience and knowledge of a sport may be helpful but are not absolutely necessary. These include positions as sportswriters and announcers, sports publicity directors, athletic trainers, and statisticians. Many people who earn a living in these jobs were never more than casual participants, yet they were hired because they had the necessary academic training or the skills — such as writing, public speaking, and working with numbers — that make them successful in their line of work.

3. Careers in ancillary industries related to sports, in which previous athletic experience is generally not important. Player representatives (agents), equipment manufacturers, food concessionaires, and employees of fitness centers and organizations that promote sports events fall into this category. Even within the management structure of a professional team, very few employees have had serious playing experience. Just check with the front office of any pro team to find out how few of its staff members have played the sport.

There are numerous athletics-related careers you may want to look into, and there is no reason that you shouldn't investigate them. However, only in coaching and scouting will your playing experience be a specific requirement for the job. For jobs in the two other sports-related categories listed above, you'll be competing with nonathletes as well as other athletes. The talents you acquired or refined as an athlete will certainly be of benefit, but they won't mean much unless you possess a variety of other generic job skills and knowledge associated with the position in question.

No matter what kind of sports-related job you may be interested in pursuing, your success will be more a function of the nonathletic skills that relate directly to the job than to any athletics-related skills you might have. If, for example, you wanted to be an agent for pro athletes, the key hiring consideration would be your talents in sales and public relations, not your previous athletics record. You can be a play-by-play announcer if you had a .210 batting average in college and a truckload of errors, but you won't make it if you have a lousy voice and don't speak English properly. Further, some of the best coaches have been among the worst athletes, and vice versa. This may be because top athletes are often naturals who don't have to think much about what they are doing on the field to do it right. In contrast, *no* coach will do well without thinking extensively about the team.

Give a sports-related occupation a chance if you really feel the need. But leave room for movement or reexamination of your career goals. Ask yourself if the sports-related occupation meets all of your needs -- in terms of income, challenge, life-style, and room for growth and advancement -- or if you are primarily taking care of your need to stay close to sports at the expense of other priorities.

Y ou can be a play-by-play baseball announcer if you had a .210 batting average in college and a truckload of errors, but you won't make it if you have a lousy voice and don't speak English properly.

Self-Defeating Patterns to Avoid

A preoccupation with athletics, especially in trying to fit it into the next phase of your life, can lead to a nonproductive and even destructive career pattern. Resist the temptation to look at your opportunities in the work world as if they had to pass through the narrow funnel of sports. You've learned from sports, but you aren't limited to work that involves sports. But before we discuss how to broaden your view of career options, let's look at the unnecessarily confining patterns that many college athletes set for their futures.

Pattern #1: "I'm going to try to make it as a pro athlete at all costs." This pattern is fueled by the immense publicity given to highly paid professional athletes. It involves continual workouts to maintain and improve physical conditioning and skills, repeated team tryouts or qualifying tournaments, and frequent contact with and referrals from coaches. These activities become all-consuming and often are done to the exclusion of any thought or effort in other career directions. Dedication is total, with thoughts of failure and what to do next vigorously pushed to the back of the athlete's mind. If you follow this pattern, you may take jobs of no consequence or ones with no opportunity for advancement while waiting for your big break. Disappointments are accepted as part of the waiting process. You draw hope from the few stories of athletes who eventually made it after long years of obscure struggle. Work harder, you say. You still have eight to ten of your body's best years ahead of you. Why waste them doing anything else besides following your dream of becoming a pro athlete?

We don't want to discourage anyone who truly has the potential to be a professional athlete. But we do want you to be aware of the likely consequence of following this pattern.

- Your college education may be curtailed and may end short of a degree. Many student-athletes who believe they have professional potential quit college soon after their eligibility expires.

- You may delay learning about other fields of work because of your preoccupation with your sport. When you eventually give up the dream of being a professional athlete, you'll have to play catch-up once you find a career that looks interesting.

- You may find your confidence withering by thinking to yourself, "If I don't make it as a pro, I won't be able to do anything." This pessimism is unnecessary and unfounded, but you may feel it because you have kept yourself from the nonathletic world of work for so long.

Pattern #2: "I'll become a great coach." Coaching is, of course, the first alternative for many athletes whose professional playing aspirations are fading. As noted earlier, it's also a career alternative strongly considered by many other college athletes who have no thought of competing as pros. Although your role as a competitive performer ends, coaching keeps you close to the competitive arena — closer to the excitement and the feeling of participation than anything else.

Keeping close to athletics through coaching often entails staying actively involved in some level of the sport, accepting any kind of coaching job no matter what the pay or level of competition, taking other jobs to supplement your income, and waiting for a break. You'll coach Pony League or Bobby Sox, junior high, anything, and push hard for a winning record to show that you're worthy of a coaching job in higher levels of competition. You'll probably continue to hope that a top coaching job will open up for you, like magic. But if you think of how many other former athletes are looking for good coaching jobs, you'll begin to understand and appreciate that getting one of these jobs is almost as difficult as competing in professional sports. You might waste many years waiting for the big break that never comes.

All former athletes believe they know well the sport they played. Many believe they can transmit this knowledge to others simply because of their experience as players. But if you don't have any appreciation for teaching and the administrative details of coaching, then you probably don't belong there. It's a good profession but a tough one, requiring a good deal of dedication. Having been a player, even a great one, is merely a starting point in the profession of coaching.

The majority of athletes who stay in coaching end up as public school coaches. If this is where your career settles, you had better like teaching children and adolescents and be prepared for very little public recognition and much hard work that has nothing to do with the glamour of collegiate or professional sports. You had better like long hours, paperwork, dealing with parents, and handling troublemakers as well as the good kids. And all this for relatively little pay. Coaching is a wonderful and stimulating career *if you really want to be a coach and teacher;* coaching is *not* a refuge for frustrated and unfulfilled former athletes who just want to stay close to their sport.

If you don't have any appreciation for teaching and the administrative details of coaching, then you probably don't belong there.

Pattern #3: "Someone will reward me for having been an athlete." A peculiar yet persistent belief of some athletes is that they will do well in their career simply because they have been athletes. They believe that people *want* athletes to succeed. Whether they were star players or not, athletes generally receive considerable attention while in college and are often admired. It's easy to understand why they feel special and might expect people to want their services later on. Mixed with the inertia that comes from having been taken care of in many ways, an athlete's feeling of specialness may encourage him or her to wait for opportunities to develop and to avoid taking responsibility for this process. This harmful behavior pattern is characterized by biding one's time, coaching here and there, maybe taking a job just because it happens to be there, and waiting for a great opportunity to come along.

Especially if college athletics has given you success, rewards, and identity, these three patterns may tempt you as your thoughts turn to your future career. No one wants to put down the torch before the flame has expired, but clinging to the past or giving in to any of these three patterns can only delay the inevitable task of finding a job that matches your interests and abilities and offers challenge and room for professional growth.

Using Athletics as an Entry into Other Careers

Although most college athletes sooner or later pursue careers unrelated to athletics, student-athletes fresh out of college often try hard to find sports-related employment. While you may not stay in the first sports-related career you decide to enter, in many cases it will be a sensible way to make the transition between college athletics and the world of employment. If your career ideas are uncertain, look into the jobs that support the elaborate structure surrounding organized sports — promotion, media communications, physiology, administration, writing, transportation, stadium construction, manufacture of equipment and clothing, and so on. As you explore these areas, you'll notice that each represents a far broader profession than simply serving athletes, sports fans, and team managers. Thus, you can use your curiosity about sports-related enterprises to discover many other occupational areas. You may win your first job in a chosen career path on the basis of your athletic background but later move into the broader profession as your interests widen. You'll discover that athletics is related to almost every major occupation or profession in some way — sports involve law, medicine, media, construction, education, finance, retail, and even politics.

A Roster of Career Possibilities

The following is a guide to careers related to sports.[2] For each field, we have indicated the nature of the work, how to gain entry to it, and where to write to obtain free information about it. Each of these careers, if you are successful in the field and choose to stay with it, will allow you to pursue your love of sports on a short-term or long-term basis. Many of these fields can be entered upon completing an undergraduate degree, though many do not require a specific college major (the expertise related to these can be learned on the job). Some of the fields require training beyond a bachelor's degree, and some do not require a degree at all (however, you'll probably perform much better in these if you have the learning skills developed in a degree program).

Applied Health and Fitness

About the Field

The range of careers in health and fitness includes managing a health spa or club, providing physical therapy for the injured or infirm, working as a nutritionist, and directing a fitness center in a business or industrial setting. Health and fitness careers tend to focus on helping the ill or injured get well or on testing levels of fitness and aiding well people at various levels of fitness to become more fit. Fostering a lifetime of active fitness is the essence of the field, rather than developing a competitive athlete.

How to Prepare for the Field

A bachelor's degree with an emphasis on physical science or therapeutic recreation is necessary for entry into this field. In some cases, a master's degree or acquisition of one in the near future is required. The Association for Fitness in Business (AFB) notes that the majority of fitness program managers earned a master's degree before being hired, although fitness program assistants are often hired with only a bachelor's degree. Certification by the American College of Sports Medicine is increasingly required for full-time employment in physical therapy and fitness positions. At the other extreme, one needn't have even a bachelor's degree to work in a health and fitness club, although without a degree pay is low, job security is minimal, and opportunities for advancement are limited. Employment opportunities are expanding in businesses, hospitals, and clinics for people well prepared in this field.

Job Titles

Exercise instructor	Exercise test tech-	Nutritionist/
Fitness instructor	nologist	Dietician
Health practitioner	Fitness program	Health spa manager
Exercise physiologist	director	Recreational
Fitness/Health	Stress management	therapist
promoter	counselor	
Physical therapist		

Information Sources

American College of Sports Medicine
P.O. Box 1440
Indianapolis, IN 46206
317-637-9200

American Physical Therapy Association
1111 North Fairfax Street
Alexandria, VA 22314
703-684-2782

Association of Physical Fitness Centers
600 Jefferson Street
Rockville, MD 20852
301-424-7744

Athletic Training

About the Field

Athletic trainers help the injured to recuperate and healthy people to stay so. When employed in a school setting, athletic trainers may also teach courses. At the high school level, just as coaches are, athletic trainers are hired primarily to teach and secondarily (for supplemental pay) to treat and prevent injuries of athletes. At the college level their primary duty is training, and their work load is filled out by teaching and, sometimes, by coaching.

In addition to taping body parts and running the training room, the athletic trainer serves as the link between the team physicians, coaches, and athletes. Trainers must attend all school athletic contests (often traveling with teams) and must be available or have an assistant available during team practices.

Athletic trainers also are employed by private sports-injury clinics. Clinic-based trainers, of course, have no teaching duties and their work schedule is more regular, although pay tends to be somewhat lower than in schools. In professional sports, athletic training jobs are extremely scarce and job security is poor (coaching changes are frequent and new coaches tend to bring their own assistants and clubhouse personnel with them).

How to Prepare for the Field

Those employed in this field carry the title athletic trainer, certified (ATC). In order to qualify for the certification exam, the candidate must have a bachelor's degree in any major, plus have either successfully completed the athletic training curriculum at one of about sixty universities approved by the National Athletic Trainers' Association (NATA) or completed a minimum 1,800 hours over at least a two-year period in a training room supervised by an ATC. In 1984, 3,400 ATCs were members of NATA. Women account for about one third of this number, and that proportion is increasing.

Job Titles

Athletic trainer	Trainer/Manager	Trainer/Teacher
Trainer/Coach	Physical therapist	Trainer-intern
Professor		

Information Source

National Athletic Trainers' Association
2952 Stemmons, Suite 200
Dallas, TX 75247-6103
800-879-6282 (toll-free)

Coach/Teacher (School Sports)

About the Field

High school coaching. Traditionally, coaches at junior and senior high schools have been full-time faculty members whose coaching duties were in addition to teaching. Recently in some states, more part-timers have been hired to coach school teams. These coaches are drawn from the ranks of substitute teachers, elementary school teachers, and people whose regular work is elsewhere.

High school coaches seldom do recruiting (except at some private schools) or fund-raising, as college coaches are expected to do, although they may be allowed (and inclined) to scout opponents. High school coaches may be involved in more than one sport, often as head coach in one sport while an assistant in another. While most scheduling of contests and hiring of officials are set by their leagues, high school coaches spend much time and energy ordering, maintaining, and storing equipment and arranging for transportation.

University and college coaching. At some large universities, coaches of revenue-producing sports may be hired just to coach.

Most college-level coaches, however, are also faculty members with coaching duties as a regular part of their job assignment. At some schools, coaches are not hired on a tenure track. That is, they have no job security and may be fired or reassigned as administrators desire.

College-level coaches teach courses, serve on committees, and advise students. Depending on the size of the college or university and the athletics program, the coaches may be responsible for equipment purchase and maintenance and travel arrangements, as well as scheduling nonleague contests and hiring officials for them. Of course, college coaches also spend much time recruiting new players and scouting opponents. The bulk of this tedious and difficult job falls to assistant coaches (if there are assistant coaches). Most of those who want to be college-level coaches should expect to spend several years doing as much or more recruiting and scouting than actual coaching as they work their way up the ranks.

How to Prepare for the Field

High school coaching. The vast majority of high school coaches not only have a bachelor's degree, but are required also to hold a teaching credential issued by the state. Some states additionally require certification of coaching knowledge and ability.

Entry-level coaching jobs tend to go to those qualified candidates who are known by more than their resume, transcript, and a brief job interview. Important contacts are often made through student teaching or referrals from the candidate's own coach.

University and college coaching. One might think that coaching at a higher level would require more academic preparation and/or additional certification, but that isn't necessarily the case in college-level coaching. Those who are hired as faculty members are often expected to obtain a master's degree, especially if they want to climb the faculty rank and pay scale. However, college-level coaches may be hired without even a bachelor's degree, and state certification requirements for teaching in higher education are rare (although less rare in community colleges). College-level coaching as a field is much like a fraternity or sorority, and many initial jobs are obtained by personal recommendation and reputation rather than objective, measurable standards.

Job Titles

Head coach	Coach administrator	Fund-raiser
Teacher/Coach	Assistant coach	Recruiter/Scout

Information Sources

American Baseball Coaches Association
P.O. Box 3545
Omaha, NE 68103-0545
402-733-0374

American Football Coaches Association
7758 Wallace Road
Orlando, FL 32819
407-351-6113

Golf Coaches Association of America
P.O. Box 8082
Statesboro, GA 30460
912-681-9100

National Association of Basketball Coaches of the U.S.
P.O. Box 307
Branford, CT 06405
203-488-1232

National Association of Intercollegiate Athletics
1221 Baltimore
Kansas City, MO 64105
816-842-5050

National Collegiate Athletic Association
U.S. Highway 50 and Nall Avenue
P.O. Box 1906
Mission, KS 66201
913-339-1906

National High School Athletic Coaches Association
P.O. Box 1808
Ocala, FL 32678
904-622-3660

National Junior College Athletic Association
P.O. Box 7305
Colorado Springs, CO 80933
719-590-9788

National Wrestling Coaches Association
c/o Athletic Department
University of Utah
Salt Lake City, UT 84112
801-581-3836

Recreation Specialist

About the Field

Employment opportunities in this field range from public-sector jobs to commercial positions, which include such varied situations as the travel and tourism industry, theme parks, large corporations that provide recreation for employees, and campground management. The beginning recreation specialist in the public sector (city and county parks and recreation departments, state and federal agencies, prisons, hospitals, etc.) is likely to supervise activities at playgrounds and indoor recreation facilities; organize, coach, and direct playground-based sports teams; stage plays; work with arts and crafts; and lead similar activities for the extremely wide age group of people who use public recreation facilities. With more experience, the recreation specialist may plan recreational programs, fund drives, and community social functions, as well as plan for, purchase, develop, and maintain open space and natural resources.

A physical health–related area of recreation work is called therapeutic recreation. Here the worker helps people who are ill, injured, or aged to rehabilitate to full activity or to adjust their level of activity to an appropriate, healthful, and enjoyable mode.

How to Prepare for the Field

Entry-level playground and recreation center workers do not need a bachelor's degree, but a junior college associate degree is helpful in landing a job. A position as a supervisor generally requires at least a bachelor's degree, while a master's degree is desirable for higher-level work. More than half of those holding chief administrator jobs in parks and recreation hold master's degrees. Recreation leaders in public schools need state certification.

In therapeutic recreation, certification is required in thirty states, with more states leaning toward it. Most certified positions appear in the public sector. The private sector is more lenient.

In commercial recreation, the two things that may be needed to find a job are personal skills and personality. But jobs are scarce, and there is a trend toward hiring candidates with more education.

Job Titles

Leisure resource specialist	Recreation therapist
Recreation supervisor	Resort activity coordinator
Therapeutic recreation specialist	Playground leader
Travel consultant	Community Center leader
Industrial recreation leader	Corrective recreation
Recreation resources manager	specialist
Recreation administrator	Camp supervisor/
Park manager	Administrator

Information Sources

American Association for Leisure and Recreation
1900 Association Drive
Reston, VA 22091
703-476-3472

National Recreation and Park Association
3101 Park Center Drive
Alexandria, VA 22302
703-820-4940

Sporting Goods Merchandising and Sales

About the Field

In addition to customer contact, retail sporting goods salespeople are involved with inventory processing and may also be expected to perform maintenance on customers' ski, tennis, golf, and other equipment. Retail sales personnel may also have considerable contact with coaches of local school and recreational teams.

Manufacturer's representatives sell to retail sporting goods stores and sometimes to teams or entire recreational leagues. Much of their time is spent traveling to meet with buyers and to attend sporting goods shows. A salesperson's reputation in athletics and a network of contacts are assets in the team sales domain. The many small sporting goods and apparel companies that have emerged with the boom in fitness and participant sports are frequently represented, not by their own salaried employees, but by independent sales agents who work strictly on commission and represent several lines of goods.

How to Prepare for the Field

Although there are no standards for educational level or experience to enter this field, employers tend to prefer those with some college background, though not necessarily a bachelor's degree.

Employment as a manufacturer's representative or independent sales agent generally cannot be considered an entry-level position, unless one's reputation as a famous athlete is enough to sell merchandise. But if the choice for someone to fill a job at this level comes down to a famous former athlete and someone who is trained and has experience in business practice and protocol, the latter is likely to get the job. Those who are employed in this field tend to be people who, over time, have developed a network of contacts in the sporting goods industry. Many have risen to this level of sales after having owned or managed retail outlets.

Job Titles

Salesperson	Equipment technician	Product developer
Pro shop manager	Retail outlet buyer	Independent sales
Manufacturer's	Store manager	agent
representative		Product-line
		promoter

Information Sources

National Sporting Goods Association
1699 Wall Street
Mount Prospect, IL 60056
708-439-4000

Sporting Goods Manufacturers Association
200 Castlewood Drive
North Palm Beach, FL 33408
407-842-4100

Sports Club and Camp Teaching/Coaching

About the Field
Amateur club sports. Tennis clubs, golf courses and driving ranges, swimming clubs, gymnastics clubs, and ski areas also offer career opportunities for teaching and coaching amateur athletes. Many of these jobs are primarily instructional in nature, while some combine instruction with the development of competitive club teams. Pay tends to be low, hours are long, and some of the jobs include peripheral duties, such as maintaining facilities, stocking and selling merchandise at the pro shop, and even drumming up business for the club.

Sports camps and summer camps. There has been great growth recently in camps for specific team sports for school-age youth and in camps for all ages in particular individual sports. This growth expands a job market that already includes summer camps for youth that encompass several sports. Most of these jobs are seasonal with low pay, unless one gets involved in the management and client-recruitment end of the business.

How to Prepare for the Field
Amateur club sports. No state certification is required for club teaching/coaching, although several sport associations either require or recommend their own certification. Whether certification is required or not, a person with certification is a more attractive job candidate. A call to a club will provide information as to the need for certification and what it entails. Experience as a college athlete is often enough for an entry-level job as a club sport teacher/coach.

Sports camps and summer camps. Experience as a college athlete is often sufficient for job entry, while certification in some sports may be recommended.

Job Titles
Head coach	Club administrator	Club teaching pro
Teacher/Coach	Assistant coach	Public relations officer

Information Source
American Camping Association
5000 State Road 67 North
Martinsville, IN 46151
317-342-8456

Sports Information

About the Field
Sports information directors (SIDs) at colleges and universities have the primary responsibility for getting the accomplishments of the teams in front of the public. Coaches rely on the SID's ability to do this well. SIDs act as the link between the media and coaches and athletes. Most of an SID's work time is spent producing and distributing media guides, press releases, brochures, and newsletters, and keeping and disseminating sports-related statistics. SIDs may also be expected to photograph contests and take team and individual pictures. In addition, the SID may be responsible for administering the press box during football and basketball games.

How to Prepare for the Field
A bachelor's degree is usually required to be an SID, and nearly one fourth of people in that position have a master's degree. The bachelor's degree should be in journalism, English, communications, or related fields. Strong communication and writing skills and the ability to organize masses of information are required, as are stamina and interest in a broad range of sports (rather than interest in only one or two sports).

Job Titles
Sports information director   Media liaison
Statistician   Public relations officer

Information Source
College Sports Information Directors of America
Texas A&I University
Box 114
Kingsville, TX 78363
512-595-3908

Sports Journalism

About the Field

Print media. A common perception about sports journalists is that they attend contests and then write about them. That is only a fragment of a sportswriter's work, especially those writers employed by small newspapers. Sportswriters also rewrite stories phoned in by stringers (writers who are paid per story), revise wire service stories to fit the newspaper's format and time frame, write advance stories and sidebars for the contests they are going to cover, and write feature articles profiling personalities and teams. At small newspapers, they are likely also to compose headlines, write photo captions, and help with proofreading and page layout.

A sports journalist's hours are extremely long and always include weekends (and frequently nights), while the pay is low — but they love it. Sports journalism is one way that a former athlete can stay close to sports, coaches, and other athletes while earning a living.

On magazines, entry-level sportswriting jobs are rare. Seldom do first-time reporters at magazines or large newspapers get to cover contests. Their work consists primarily of rewriting press releases, piecing together wire service copy, conducting research for more established writers, and doing filing and other clerical chores.

Radio and television. Despite the proliferation of sports shows and sports networks, there are still relatively few jobs in electronic sports journalism. Those who do appear on the air tend to be either trained and experienced journalism majors or recognizable former players and coaches. If there is a place for former college athletes who know a lot about sports, it is as research assistants for the on-air personalities. There is tedium in this work, little room for advancement, and little glamour.

How to Prepare for the Field

To begin a career in sports journalism, a bachelor's degree is usually required, although not necessarily a major in journalism. An English or liberal arts major is also attractive to employers because these areas require writing, thinking, and personal organization skills.

The best way to break into the field is to do part-time journalism work (certainly on the school newspaper or radio and/or TV station) while in college, then, after graduating, seek a job at a small newspaper or local station where a wide array of duties will be required, thus making you more marketable later. Prospective employers may want to see samples of your writing or audio or video tapes. A portfolio of bylined articles to show prospective employers should always be kept.

Job Titles

Sportswriter	Research assistant	Editorial clerk
Columnist	Reporter	Stringer
Editor		

Information Sources

American Sportscasters Association
150 Nassau Street
New York, NY 10038
212-227-8080

National Sportscasters and Sportswriters Association
P.O. Drawer 559
Salisbury, NC 28144
704-633-4275

The Newspaper Fund
P.O. Box 300
Princeton, NJ 08543
609-452-2820

Sports Scientist (Academic)

About the Field

Sports scientists who work in an academic setting study all aspects of sports—from the athletes' bodies and performance to behaviors of athletes, coaches, and fans. They may study the history of sports or how sports appear in other cultures. Each area of sports science operates from a particular academic discipline. For example, biomechanics focuses on the efficiency of human movement, sport sociology is the study of how athletes and athletics reflect or deviate from the culture, and sport psychology considers a range of behaviors including how people learn to move and the methods for training and motivating athletes.

Academic sports scientists may also teach college-level courses in their field of study. As faculty members they have other duties, including committee work and student advising. At many schools they are also expected to publish and/or win research grants.

How to Prepare for the Field

Academic sports scientists have at least a master's degree and have or are planning to earn a doctorate. A recent sample of thirty-six sport psychologists indicated that twenty-six held a doctorate, while six of the eight who held only a master's degree were seeking a doctorate. In this small sample, physical education was the predominant undergraduate major (held by twenty of the thirty-six), while eight held degrees in social science area and eight held degrees in some other field.

Job Titles

Sport sociologist   Sport psychologist   Exercise physiologist
Sport anthropologist   Sport historian   Biomechanicist

Information Sources

North American Society for Sport History
101 White Building
Pennsylvania State University
University Park, PA 16802
814-865-2416

North American Society for the Psychology of Sport
    and Physical Activity
131 Esslinger Hall
University of Oregon
Eugene, OR 97403
503-346-4108

North American Society for the Sociology of Sport
Department of Physical Education
University of Illinois
Champaign, IL 61820
217-333-6563

We have presented detailed information about sports careers in this chapter because detailed descriptions of such careers and how to enter the related fields are hard to come by. Remember, though, that many of the skills that you can develop in sports-related careers will help you get ahead in fields not connected to sports. For instance:

- A good salesperson of sports equipment can use sales skills to sell *any* product or service.
- A sportswriter can apply journalistic writing skills to many other writing fields. Furthermore, writing ability is highly valued and often lacking in candidates for upper management in the business world and elsewhere.
- An athletic director can apply management skills to any organization that needs strong leadership and movement toward its goals.
- A fitness center manager or owner can apply business skills to the running of any profit-making enterprise or nonprofit organization.

Careers Outside of Sports

An athlete who graduates with a college degree can enter *any* field of work that he or she chooses. The sports-related careers noted in the preceding section represent only a small part of the broad spectrum that constitutes the world of work. A strategy can be developed to pursue any job in the business, government, nonprofit, or educational sectors that a graduate-athlete may desire.

Many nonsports career plans cannot be developed by athletes until after they have graduated. Often the athlete doesn't have enough time or motivation during college to investigate a nonsports career. It's even less likely that the student-athlete can gain experience in a nonsports field while in college because sports seasons, training camps, and the like often get in the way.

Regardless of when you begin your plan for a career outside of sports, your entry route will be found in one of two broad categories.

1. A career in which technical training is required. Such training would be acquired during college (for example, in an

engineering or pharmacy program) or in a graduate or professional school in such fields as law, psychology, architecture, social work, and environmental science.

2. A nontechnical career that can be entered with an undergraduate degree regardless of the major field of study. In such fields, which include a wide range of for-profit and nonprofit kinds of work, general learning skills would be used to acquire knowledge and techniques on the job.

Some career fields outside of sports do not require a college degree, but these are few. Increasingly, employers require or prefer that new employees in professional positions have a college education.

Eventually, most athletes who graduate from college enter fields of work that are not sports related. Many may try a sports career first, but expand their horizons later on. How do so many former athletes make productive transitions to careers that have little to do with their main involvement as college students?

- As noted in an earlier chapter, the typical athlete qualities of discipline, team orientation, and goal directedness make a hardworking and achievement-oriented employee.

- Success in athletics breeds a winning attitude that carries over to the competitiveness of the business world and to the result orientation of many careers.

- As college graduates, former athletes bring with them generic learning skills that enable them to learn new jobs quickly and adapt to a variety of work requirements.

- In many career fields, employers are pleased to find new talent and train these people for positions of leadership in their organizations—especially when the graduate is highly motivated and willing to learn a new field from the ground up.

Dozens of sports-related careers and hundreds more that have little or nothing to do with sports are available to the student-athlete who graduates with a college degree. You can enter any of these fields and prosper according to your special talents and level of motivation. Athletics do not in any way dictate the career you should enter; your experiences will provide you with qualities that can be used in any line of work. An informal survey of the job market reveals former athletes in business, government, science, education, the arts, human services, entrepreneurship, and every other corner of the employed world. Choose the career that looks most challenging, and we are confident that your athletics background will be an asset in whatever you do.

11

Strategies for Winning the Job You Want

Develop a Network of Contacts . . .
Assess Your Strengths . . . Skills Scorecards . . .
How to Get Interviews and Do Well at Them . . .
Strategies for Winning

Successful job hunting requires a combination of three factors: connecting yourself to people in the world of work, deciding what your strengths are and the jobs to which you want to apply them, and obtaining job interviews and communicating your assets effectively.

As a student-athlete, you can perform well in all three dimensions of the job search. You have many potential contacts who can help you identify opportunities in the job world. You have many personal strengths and attributes derived from sports that are valuable to employers. And you have the ability and competitiveness to perform well in job interviews. In this chapter you'll learn how to take best advantage of the many qualities that you already possess for effective job hunting.

Develop a Network of Contacts

Although you can obtain interviews in many ways, by far the most productive source of informal or formal job information will come from people you know who refer you to people they know. Talking with people in person—whether they have jobs open or not—is perhaps the single most important step in the job search.

177

By plugging into one cell of a network of contacts in any field of work, you open up your potential to meet many people because of the connections—personal, professional, or both—that exist among them. All college students have a primary set of contacts they can tap—relatives, neighbors, faculty, friends, parents of friends—but it is your good fortune that student-athletes tend to start off with many more contacts than the average student. This is because there is a large, informal alliance of former athletes and a horde of sports fans in virtually every field of work.

Many people who have played or followed sports feel a common bond with you and are likely to have a genuine desire to give you access to the work world—that all-important first chance—that every job seeker needs. For reasons that we don't fully understand, people in this network generalize their own athletic involvement (as fan, participant, or both) to an affection for all athletes. It's as though you belong to an immense fraternity-sorority in which you hold life membership.

Questions to Ask Your Contacts

The point of developing contacts is *not* to immediately ask for a job from the person you meet. Remember, this isn't a job interview. The first contact should be to exchange information—you ask about the field of work, and your contact asks questions about you and your plans. Your information gathering will generally be in one of the three following areas.

General nature of the work. Typical questions to ask might include "What kind of work do you do? What kind of qualities do you look for in an employee? What are the rewards and pressures of this field?"

Entry routes. Questions include "How might I get into this field of work? What kinds of training or experience would you recommend? How can I get an edge on the competition?" The people you talk to know their field of work from the inside. Learn from their experience.

Nature of specific jobs. Questions include "What is involved in your particular job? How does it fit with the organization? How can I work toward a job like yours?" People like to talk about themselves. Use this to your advantage. You may even find that these information-gathering sessions propel you further into the network. It's not unusual to have the person you are talking with get on the phone and say, "I've got someone here who is interested in what you folks are doing. Why don't you two get together?"

How do you present yourself to people in your network? Do you just say, "Hi there, I played college hoops?" No! If you were referred by a coach or other athletics-related person, the contact will probably already know what sport you played and will open the conversation that way. However, if the contact doesn't mention it, you may include this information in your introduction of yourself, but soft-pedal it from there and rapidly move on to the real focus of your meeting.

If you are not sure the person knows you have been an athlete or has any special interest in athletics, simply include the relevant information on your resume and mention it during the general conversation in connection with job qualifications ("I learned to commit myself to a team effort in basketball and recognize that teamwork is important here in your organization"). It's okay to mention your athletics background when contacts ask you to talk about yourself, but don't try to impress them with it. Let them form their own conclusions.

Assess Your Strengths

As you review your particular strengths and unique attributes, you'll be pleased to know that athletics breeds special qualities that sports participants can use to their advantage when job hunting. Part of selling yourself is to recognize these assets in yourself and to talk about them as part of your total qualifications.

Competing in a college sport makes you different from most other college students in that you have already acquired work experience — as a team member — in addition to the tasks you performed as a student. In many ways, competing on a team comes closer to mirroring the characteristics of existing in the work world than anything else most students do during their years of higher education. When a coach says, "This player gets the job done," the allusion to working life is not accidental. The coach means that the player has trained hard, listened and learned through supervision, integrated his or her tasks with others (important even in individual sports), and shown loyalty, and could be counted on for ongoing participation. In short, the player has met many of the requirements of modern organizational life and has a running start on fitting into the workplace.

We regard athletes as good candidates for highly de-manding positions in industry, because they were able to fit the pressures of athletics into a busy academic schedule. Athletes are able to organize their time well, they have exceptionally high energy, and they are dedi-cated to accomplishing their goals. In addition, they have a lot of tenacity. We like the balance that athletes offer; they demonstrate they can handle several respon-sibilities at once.

Michael Ippolito, manager, corporate recruiting, International Paper Company

---

It is in the nature of athletics to impart the following ten quali-ties to team players. These personal strengths are desirable in virtually all jobs, regardless of the field.

- *Ability to organize time well.* Athletes are often outstanding in apportioning their time because they must balance a full-time academic work load, full-time commitment to athletics, travel to other schools for games, time out for fatigue, and possibly part-time employment or other off-campus com-mitments. Take a close look at the different activities you have juggled during college, and appreciate the time-management skills you have developed as a result.

- *Ability to work well with others.* Through athletic team mem-bership, most athletes become intimately familiar with the experience of working toward group goals. Working with a coach is a lot like working with a department manager. The dynamics of team play teaches the athlete what it means to be a role player — that it is sometimes necessary to submerge one's ego and personal goals into the goals of the organiza-tion — and that leadership is the ability to get people to work as a team.

- *Goal directedness.* Athletes cultivate the ability to concentrate their energies and attention over an extended period of time and to block out distractions while they proceed toward their goal. Every athlete knows that this directedness is the key to all accomplishments.

- *Competitiveness.* The competitive spirit is the lifeblood of the athletics experience, and most athletes thrive on it. They gain experience in the rigors of winning and losing, and they relish the opportunity to fight more battles, test their abilities, and risk their self-esteem against tough opposition. This translates into a strong asset in most jobs.

- *Confidence.* Athletes are continually in situations where they must pump themselves up and believe in their own power to produce effectively under pressure. The ability to approach tough performance situations with the belief that you'll do well is crucial. Practice in maintaining self-confidence, especially under tense circumstances, can carry over to stiff on-the-job challenges.

- *Persistence and endurance.* Athletics is often characterized by long and hard work toward distant rewards and the ability to wring a maximum effort from yourself whenever necessary. This may include playing while in pain or, in general, performing under adverse circumstances. Athletics teaches intensity of effort and the belief that sufficient preparation and determination will eventually pay off.

- *Loyalty.* Closely related to the ability to work as part of a team, loyalty emerges from the bond that an individual athlete builds with his or her team and is expressed in the willingness to support team efforts under any circumstances. Loyalty contributes heavily to the morale of a team or work group, because it enables each team member to trust that others will work toward the same ends.

- *Discipline.* Discipline is a hallmark of the athletics experience. Organizing one's time, adhering to guidelines, exacting maximum effort on a regular basis, concentrating one's energies, and screening out competing priorities are all necessary for competence in athletics. The systematic application of one's energies toward a desired goal is highly valued in any work situation, especially in those that require independent effort.

- *Ability to take criticism.* Athletes are accustomed to taking criticism, because their performance on the field is watched closely; any weak points seldom escape comment. Coaches recommend changes and force athletes to cope with the feeling that they could've done better. Athletes typically develop into good listeners when constructive criticism is offered, because they recognize its value in helping them advance toward overall goals.

- *Resilience.* Sports offer continued opportunities to test oneself, succeed or fail, and then come back for more. No one who competes in a sport can avoid the experience of failure. Athletes learn, by necessity, to face failure and bury any negative feelings as much and as soon as possible because tomorrow's contest will require their full attention. Among the most valuable lessons of athletics are how to win, how to lose, and how to rebound from both.

We don't expect that all college athletes will have developed in great abundance all ten of the qualities noted here. Many athletes will look at these descriptions of qualities and say, "That's not me." Nonetheless, it's likely that you have more of these qualities than most nonathletes do, and we believe you should appreciate them in yourself and use them to your advantage.

Expressing Your Strengths as Skills

Every job requires two kinds of skills: job-specific skills (those that one trains for or learns on the job) and functional skills (generic skills that cut across many different jobs). The difference between the two can be illustrated in an occupational example. A radio announcer must possess the job-specific skills necessary to operate the dials at the station and must also be able to speak well, manage time carefully, and relate easily to the public. Unlike job-specific skills, functional skills transcend job titles and are applicable to a wide variety of occupations.

The functional skills listed below are needed in a broad array of jobs across many industries and professions. In reviewing the list, consider how many of these skills you possess.

- *Writing:* communicating clearly and persuasively in written reports, letters, and other verbal formats.
- *Public speaking:* delivering talks, fielding questions, speaking on the spur of the moment, and participating in public forums with relative ease.
- *Supervising:* overseeing the work performance of others by observing their work firsthand, making recommendations for improvements, clarifying performance goals, resolving problems, and rendering disciplinary actions (when necessary).
- *Organizing people:* coordinating projects and programs that involve the efforts of others so that people work effectively together.
- *Organizing data:* putting together quantitative and other information logically and effectively.
- *Research:* using printed materials and other resources to investigate and gather information on particular topics in coherent form.
- *Quantitative skills:* using and understanding the numerical methods needed to analyze problems and suggest solutions.
- *Computer skills:* using personal computers and word processing programs and comprehending and contributing to the design of logical systems of information flow, including knowledge of hardware and/or the ability to write or understand software programs.
- *Persuading:* using spoken communication, written words, or media to influence the opinions and attitudes of others.
- *Managing:* developing policies toward organizational objectives and allocating tasks to individuals so that the objectives can be realized.
- *Teaching:* explaining and helping individuals or groups of people to understand concepts, procedures, and other kinds of information.
- *Imagination:* developing and using creative, innovative approaches to the solution of problems.

Other important functional skills include planning, negotiating, relating to the public, handling detail, resolving conflicts, interviewing, counseling, selling, and delegating responsibility.

The Importance of Communication Skills

On the preceding list of skills that are highly potent in every job market, writing and speaking stand out. Although only a small number of college graduates will take jobs as writers or be in positions that require frequent public speaking, basic competency in both writing and speaking is crucial to job success across the board.

Communication skills are not given at birth; they are acquired. You can improve your writing and speaking skills by using them. If you know you are a poor writer, take courses that require term papers (this is the most useful suffering you may ever endure in school) and write letters to your friends — in short, do whatever it takes to cultivate better writing skills.

No matter how much technical knowledge you may have acquired in a particular job area, your advancement potential will depend heavily upon your ability to communicate in writing and in speech. Successful executives know their subject matter and can talk or write about it to anyone.

If I could choose one degree for the people I hire, it would be English. I want people who can read and speak in the language we're dealing with. You can teach a group of Cub Scouts to do portfolio analysis.

A senior vice president
of the First Atlanta Corporation [1]

Skills Scorecards

In any given field of work, the success of your job search may depend upon your ability to clarify your skills with respect to the particular job you are seeking. You'll state your qualifications in your resume and in the cover letters you send to prospective employers. Later you'll talk about these same qualifications in job interviews. When an interviewer asks: "Why should we hire you?" you should be prepared to answer in terms of both your track record of accomplishments (your academic background and work experiences) and your skills.

Develop the habit of interpreting your experiences in terms of skills. By doing so, you'll be able to assess your potential for any job. The best way to convince yourself and others that you possess a particular skill is to name it and tell how you acquired it.

Example: I am good at supervising people.

I developed this skill in my job as a ranch foreman during the summers and as cocaptain of my school's basketball team.

The Skills Scorecards on the following two pages illustrate a simple approach athletes can use to review their academic and nonacademic experiences and identify the skills they have acquired. This information can then be used to support your particular employment goals, both in discussions with interviewers and in the written materials (your resume and cover letters) you send in your job search.

In constructing your own Skills Scorecard, you'll see that as a student-athlete you have developed certain skills in sports and others in nonathletic activities. All of these skills contribute to your overall career potential. Sports participation gives you a head start on certain skills but cannot provide all the skills you'll need for your intended career. Therefore, it pays to examine the whole range of your activities, as shown in the preceding examples. Very often, even if the career you're interested in seems far removed from your background, you'll be able to identify skills in your athletic and nonathletic experiences that will support your career goal and make you a viable candidate for jobs in that field.

Athlete Profile

Applying Lessons from Coach to the Outside World

Jack Collins is one of thousands who taste success in college football but who quickly discover that there's little chance of a professional career in their future. Halfback on the state championship team during high school and star offensive back for the University of Texas at Austin from 1958 until 1962, Collins had one year of professional football with the Pittsburgh Steelers and then found himself on the Dallas Cowboys taxi

---

Skills Scorecard No. 1

List all your experiences on and off the field

Sport:	Football
Off-field athletic activity:	Coaching at special education center
Academic major:	History
Campus activity:	Fraternity officer
Off-season jobs:	Volunteer in political campaign, camp counselor

Analyze each experience in terms of skills required

Experience	Skill
Football	Determination, teamwork, self-discipline
Football, coaching, fraternity	Motivating group to action
Coaching, political campaign	Attention to detail
Coaching, counselor	Teaching, developing patience
History major	Writing
History major, political campaign	Research, organizing data
Fraternity	Running meetings, mediating conflicts
Political campaign	Polling and analyzing results

What possible careers have you considered?

Public relations	Public interest group coordinator
Political aide	Paralegal

Evaluate how the skills you have identified can be used in a given career

Public relations:	Writing, organizing data, research
Political aide:	Teamwork, research, organizing data, writing, mediating conflicts, planning events, motivating group to action, attention to detail, polling and analyzing results
Public interest group coordinator:	Research, organizing data, writing, determination, teamwork, running meetings, mediating conflicts, motivating group to action, teaching, attention to detail, polling and analyzing results
Paralegal:	Research, organizing data, writing, attention to detail

Skills Scorecard No. 2

List all your experiences on and off the field

Sport:	Track, swimming
Off-field athletic activity:	Players' Committee
Academic major:	English
Campus activities:	Sports reporter for campus newspaper, sports commentator for campus radio station
Off-season jobs:	Helped set up community joggers club, summer lifeguard

Analyze each experience in terms of skills acquired

Experience	Skill
Track, swimming	Self-discipline, self-motivation
Track, swimming, radio commentator	Time budgeting
Track, swimming, radio commentator, lifeguard	Concentration
Track, swimming, Players' Committee, reporter	Perseverance
Players' Committee	Negotiating ability, problem solving
Players' Committee, radio commentator	Public speaking
Players' Committee, setting up joggers club	Organizing
English major, reporter	Writing, analytical ability
Reporter, radio commentator	Interviewing

What possible careers have you considered?

Journalism
Radio or TV commentator
Advertising

Evaluate how the skills you have identified can be used in a given career

Journalism:	Self-discipline, self-motivation, time budgeting, perseverance, writing, analytical ability, interviewing
Radio or TV commentator:	Time budgeting, concentration, public speaking, writing, analytical ability, interviewing
Advertising:	Concentration, perseverance, problem solving, organizing

squad. At that point, he realized he had to think of something else to do besides football.

Collins became president of the First City Bank in Austin, Texas, a growing bank in one of the fastest-growing cities in the country. How did he prepare for such a career? Collins looks back on his years of observing his coach, Darrell Royal, one of the most successful college football coaches of all time: "I noticed how Coach Royal was a master at organizing everything, and particularly at placing people in the right roles, getting the most out of everyone. I think that I have remembered a lot of those lessons in my work as a manager and executive with the bank."

So, while Darrell Royal was putting together one of the premium organizations in collegiate sports, young Jack Collins was watching. He took his first job with Republic Bank in Dallas, worked there for ten years, and then was hired by First City Bank in Austin as a senior vice president in the mid 1970s. "I learned from Coach Royal the importance of letting staff do their job, whether defensive line coach or head of the loan department," Collins recalls.

Collins also cites discipline and the ability to manage time as qualities that college athletes acquire and that help them in their careers. Remembering his own experience, he notes, "We could not cut any classes without a legitimate excuse. One Wednesday morning at 6 a.m. I found myself running steps at the stadium because I had missed a class. I learned to take discipline, manage my time, and become a disciplinarian myself. Nowadays, when a guy comes late to our staff meetings at the bank, I feel it's important to let him know it – in front of everyone else."

When Collins talks about his and the bank's goals for the future, the sports metaphors fly: "We have a team goal for the bank – to become the largest bank in Austin. In order to reach this goal, we have to have a game plan, and we need the right type of people to work that plan."

Clearly, Collins relishes the competitive atmosphere that exists among banks in the area and feels comfortable in building game plans that will gain an edge on the opposition.

How to Get Interviews and Do Well at Them

To be as professional as possible, it's necessary to follow certain codes of behavior that are standard, accepted practices in job hunting. There are five areas of the job-winning game: (1) making the initial contact, (2) dressing appropriately, (3) preparing for the interview, (4) handling the interview, and (5) using your resume and cover letter.

Making the Initial Contact

- Call whoever in an organization is responsible for the department you'd like to work in and ask for an interview. State the specific position you desire. Be organized. Through research you should have discovered whom to call and the particular jobs he or she is responsible for.

- Be prepared to recount your qualifications for the job over the telephone if you are asked.

- If the secretary of the department head refers you to the personnel department, call there for an interview, but ask if you may speak to the department head as well.

- You may precede your call by sending your resume and a cover letter, but that is not required. Don't depend upon a resume and letter to stimulate an employer to invite you for an interview.

- Precede any request for an interview with the name of the person who referred you (if any): "___ recommended that I call you."

- If the organization's hiring officials cannot grant you an interview, ask where they recommend that you apply. State your qualifications so they can make an appropriate referral.

- Walk in. If other approaches frustrate you, use the most direct method of all. Go to employers without an appointment. It will work better in small organizations, where hiring procedures are often less formal. Dress appropriately wherever you go. With persistence and some advance research, you should be able to get at least three walk-in interviews in a day.

Dressing Appropriately

Remember that any in-person contact, no matter how informal, requires that you dress suitably. It conveys your seriousness of purpose about the work you are seeking. In order to have your appearance count in your favor, know in advance how the people in your target organization dress, and be sure you are appropriately dressed for the position you are applying for. Be conservative but not dull. Good dress does not call attention to itself. What shows is neatness, fit with the environment of the place of work, and tastefulness. Flashiness in colors, fabric designs, jewelry, or clothing styles is out of place and distracting. If you fit in comfortably with the way people dress at your potential workplace, that will make a positive statement about your suitability for the job.

Preparing for the Interview

- Perhaps the most common job-hunting error made by college graduates is the failure to prepare for job interviews. Interviewers expect you to be interested in them and well versed in their organization. You can increase your knowledge by reading the organization's literature closely and also by learning about how recent developments in the outside world have affected the field (check the newspaper and magazine guides in the library).

- Be sure you can talk about yourself clearly and concisely in terms of your qualifications and your interest in the job and in the organization. Be fully prepared to answer why you want this particular job and why you believe you can do well in it.

- Have available a portfolio of any materials that are relevant to your past experiences. This should include a copy of your resume and might also include brochures of programs you have organized, papers you have written relevant to the job, reference letters, and job descriptions of positions you have held.

Handling the Interview

- Be sure to tell the interviewer what you want him or her to know about your qualifications. Your *main agenda* for any job interview is to establish at least three reasons why you believe you are a good candidate for this job.

  Example: I believe that I can do the job of production manager well because:

    1. I have the ability to get people to work hard.

2. I have the competitive attitude necessary for success in business.

3. I organize myself well and can get a lot of tasks done in a short period of time.

- Be early and alert for any interview—formal or informal. Take time to look around the workplace, if you can do so without prying.

- Answer questions concisely but with enough detail to be clear and accurate.

- Ask questions about the nature of the work, the growth potential in the position, expectations of your performance, and other questions that show you are evaluating the job as well as being evaluated.

- Listen carefully to the interviewer's questions and statements, and ask for clarification whenever necessary.

- Don't be stiff in your behavior. Professionalism means being well organized and motivated but not artificial in your manner.

- Ask if you may meet with others whose work is related to the job for which you are applying

Using Your Resume and Cover Letter

Some experts believe that the resume is used primarily to eliminate candidates and should therefore not be shown until an applicant has had a chance to state his or her own case in person. However, you may be requested to submit one in advance in order to be considered at all, in which case you have no choice.

- Seek advice regarding the layout, content, and printing of your resume from your college's career development or placement office before you commit yourself to its final form.

- Have your resume typeset or printed on a laser printer.

- Always have your cover letter typed as an original—not typeset or copied.

- Make sure that your resume and cover letter are well written and that the grammar and spelling are correct. Poor writing is a common reason for immediate elimination.

- A cover letter should always accompany a resume that is mailed, but a letter alone can also be used. Whether you send a letter or both items, be sure they are addressed to an individual *by name and title*. If you don't know the person's title, use his or her name only, but never write to a title without a name; this suggests that you didn't do the proper research.
- Always follow up a letter and/or resume with a phone call in which you request an interview.
- Always have a resume available during an interview, even if you sent one in advance. It's best to have several copies available.

In the samples of a resume and cover letter on the following two pages, note that Randall Athlete is a good candidate for a sales position at XYZ Corporation because of his competitiveness, sales experience, and demonstrated productivity. The jobs, activities, and experiences on his resume support these qualities, which are crucial to success in sales and marketing work. It's important that he include the skills section in his resume, so that employers will see at a glance why he considers himself to be a good candidate.

Randall's cover letter, which will accompany the resume he sends to his prospective employer, allows him to state in his own words that he believes his experiences have prepared him to do the job, even though he didn't major in business while in college. His letter is straightforward and confident, reaffirming the skills highlighted in his resume.

While not all student-athletes will have skills and experiences as well aligned with their desired job as Randall, it's important that you use your cover letter and resume to state why you believe you can do the job you're applying for. In the process, be sure to refer to whatever skills you believe are relevant.

Strategies for Winning

Unlike sports contests, *more* than half of the contestants can win in the job market. A lot of people lose simply because they are aimless and passive. The following principles call for *initiative,* which you must have if you're going to put a career game plan into action. We've used football as a metaphor for the game plan we present here, but we're sure you can translate the ideas into the

RANDALL ATHLETE

Campus Address   Permanent Address

Kinsolving Hall — 134   36 Willow Street
University of Texas   Dallas, TX 75200
Austin, TX 78700   214-555-7710
512-555-1819

Job Objective: Sales and marketing position for a consumer goods
organization

SKILLS RELEVANT TO JOB OBJECTIVE

Selling: In my summer jobs and fund-raising job on campus,
I have developed my ability to sell products and
ideas effectively to a wide variety of clients.

Competitiveness: My four years as a member of the varsity tennis teams
have sharpened my natural competitiveness and
motivated me to seek a position in a competitive
business atmosphere.

Productivity: In four years of meeting the demands of academic
and athletics schedules, concurrent with raising
money and being an officer for my fraternity, I have
learned how to perform at maximum capacity
despite many pressures. In particular, I have learned
how to manage time effectively, to deal with conflict,
and to persuade and supervise others.

EXPERIENCE

Summer 1990   *Salesman, Star Hotel Corporation* — sold travel
packages to companies in the Dallas area
Summer 1988–89   *Assistant Manager, John Doe Company* — managed
farm equipment sales to local customers
1987–90   *Fund-raising Chairman, Alpha Beta
Fraternity* — sold advertisements for fraternity
yearbook; raised $10,000 in funds during a single
year.

CAMPUS ACTIVITIES
1987–90   Men's Varsity Tennis Team
1988–90   Vice President, Alpha Beta Fraternity

EDUCATION   University of Texas at Austin
Bachelor of Arts, 1991
Major — History

Courses relevant to job objective
  Business Administration   Labor Economics
  Marketing Management   History of the Corporation
  Introduction to Computer   International Economics
    Science

REFERENCES   Available upon request

May 1, 1991

Mr. James H. Johnson
Executive Vice President
XYZ Corporation
Chicago, IL 60611

Dear Mr. Johnson:

During the past month, I've had the opportunity to read a great deal about your company. I was particularly impressed with the sales growth you have achieved and with the new products you have brought to market.

I am writing this letter to you because I am interested in working for a company like XYZ. In particular, a position with your sales organization would be extremely challenging and an important step forward from my previous experience.

Most recently, I sold travel packages to corporations that use these tours to improve their business prospects. In making these sales, I had to be highly competitive, work under considerable pressure, and show confidence in my product.

Both in the travel sales job and in my previous work selling farm equipment for John Doe Company, I dealt effectively with my customers and produced results that were praised by my superiors. I enjoy selling and want to continue in this line of work, because the challenge of selling a good product appeals to me.

I feel that my personal qualities of determination and resourcefulness enable me to perform well in sales and marketing work. During college I handled the responsibility of varsity tennis, part-time jobs, and a difficult course of study. I work harder than others do because I am ambitious and goal oriented. In particular, intercollegiate athletic competition taught me how to deal successfully with pressure and challenging situations, and how to direct myself toward tangible and worthwhile goals.

I will call next week to arrange an appointment with you, so that we may discuss job opportunities with your organization. Thank you for your time and consideration.

Sincerely,

Randall Athlete

Randall Athlete

terminology of your own sport. You are going to become your own coach, so get out the Xs and Os and you're on your way.

Know Where the Goal Line Is

Imagine being in a distance run, not knowing where you are going, how much time has elapsed, or how far you have gone. What's more, the coach won't tell you when you'll get to stop. That's what working without a goal is like. Energy is always best used for a purpose. What do you want to accomplish in your life? What would you regard as a worthy objective? The more concretely you can state: "*This* is what I am aiming for," the better your entire game plan will be.

Name your goals as concretely as possible.

- I want to run a successful small business.
- I want to become a lawyer who represents professional athletes.
- I intend to make $100,000 a year in the financial world.
- I want to be a successful coach at a small college.
- I hope to become a radio announcer for a big-city station.
- I want to win statewide election to public office.
- I want to be a top software programmer for a leading computer company.

Assemble Your Tools

Look at *everything* you know about yourself. Make a list of your attributes that you regard as positive, regardless of how remote they may seem for what you imagine to be the work setting.

Example: I'm good with my hands
I have a lot of endurance
I laugh easily
I'm good with children
I'm loyal to others
I'm careful about getting details correct

Ask your friends to add qualities to this list, because they will know aspects of talents you possess that you either deny through modesty or are completely unaware of because they come naturally to you.

195

Become aware of the skills and attributes you possess that will serve your stated goals. You want to be a financial wizard and you are good with numbers. That's a good start. Are there other skills you need for a particular career but don't have? You can work toward developing the skills in which you might be weak. The job market encourages personal development and growth. You want to be in journalism but need help with your writing style? You hope to be a teacher but don't speak very well in front of groups? Writing and speaking skills can be *acquired* through additional study and experience; build these skills to serve your career goals. Move forward armed with skills you possess and the determination to build those you don't have.

Scout the Opposition

You are not only the coach of your game plan, but you are also the scouting staff. Just as an athletic team feasts on good information about the opposition, so a well-developed career feeds off informed intelligence gathering. Your game plan will wallow in uncertainty if you have little real knowledge about the fields of work you are contemplating or fail to discover the many kinds of work suited to you and your skills. If you want to get into the film industry, get to know a good deal more about it than the bus schedule to Hollywood. Make it your business to find out about the many kinds of films that are made and the many organizations that make them (such as corporations, government agencies, and service organizations); *then* go out to Hollywood with some professional exposure to sell instead of just your dreams.

In career counseling terms, scouting is called job research. This research yields three basic kinds of information about a prospective job.

1. The nature of the work in this general category.
2. The kinds of settings these people work in: the physical arrangements, work relationships, etc.
3. The personalities in the organization who do that job and with whom you might be working.

Information about the first two items can be found in printed materials; specific knowledge of the personalities can be obtained only by personal visits.

Throw Long on First Down

A game plan is incomplete without a trick up your sleeve or a special play that exceeds normal caution. Take a goal of yours that others may label as unrealistic and try it anyway. Act boldly. If you see a career possibility that appears to be a long shot but that appeals to you, find out how others got there, and then push in that direction. What is the worst that might happen to you? You aren't likely to get trampled by a herd of wild buffalo or have a building fall on you. Whatever the consequence of failing might be, the regret that you never tried for something you really wanted would be far worse.

Just as every football fan likes the attempted long-bomb pass, those in the job market admire the guts and daring of people who set distant goals. A million bucks, a Ph.D., a screen test, a pilot's license, a business of your own, becoming manager of a skydiving club? Why not try it? The sooner you test yourself against something big, the more you will know about where your game is headed next and which abilities need more work.

Take What the Defense Gives You

Some of those "throwing long on first down" plays will not work out as you had hoped. You may not get hired by the major corporation, the deal for a business partnership may fall through, or you may not make it as a writer with a prominent magazine. What should you do when the results come in? Don't let your dreams die forever, but rather decide what you will do in the meantime.

If you miss a big opportunity, often it's not your abilities that failed. For instance, what if you have talent for the goals that you seek, but the market closed you off; there's too much competition for the role you want most; the product you hitch yourself to doesn't sell as well as hoped; or the market is not ready for what you have to offer? Try again later. Public preferences and needs change, *you* change, your product improves.

You must obey market pressures, even if they force you into a less thrilling line of work. In football, if the opposition denies the pass, you have to run. But in career development, if you miss an opportunity in one field or organization, there is usually something similar nearby. You may have wanted to sell stocks and bonds, but brokerage houses weren't interested. Seek out jobs in

197

other financial institutions, such as banks or insurance companies. If you wanted to open a restaurant but it didn't work, try another small business where prospects are better. Remember, it's all right to make a mistake. Like fumbles, errors, and turnovers, they are part of the game.

Spot the Secondary Receivers

Successful game plans, like passing attacks, flow from a many-sided probing of the opposition. Understanding that many fields of work are potentially open to you is a key to your eventual success. Knowing that you have multiple possibilities helps to lower the general anxiety associated with job hunting; having alternatives seems to be a great confidence builder.

How do you mount a multiple attack?

- Investigate many fields of work and assume there's a way into each of them for you unless and until you are *convinced* otherwise.
- Identify the key skills you possess that cut across occupational boundaries.
- Consider the entire cluster of related occupations if you are closed out of one field of work.

Example: If you want to be in advertising, but it's too competitive at the start, try public relations, marketing research, audiovisual work, media research, and other fields directly relevant to the advertising industry.

Having multiple targets is very practical, because it means that you are seldom stuck for new ideas. The broader the areas in which you can imagine your skills being used, the more powerful your attack.

Example: If you like teaching, but a teaching job isn't available, take some of the personal attributes that led you to like teaching (enjoying interpersonal contact, being a leader, having a sense of command, being outgoing), and apply them to counseling, sales, personnel work, lobbying in government, and so on.

Teachers may not always be in great demand, but the skills that go into teaching always are.

The Two-Minute Drill

A two-minute drill in football practice teaches a team to be its most coordinated and to use its best plays under time pressure and with little direction from the bench. Similarly, you must be ready to perform as a job candidate at any moment. Looking for work is an unpredictable, disorderly process. You may run across a career possibility when you least expect it. You may meet a person on a train or have dinner with a friend's mother and discover that these people can offer you an opportunity.

Unlike football, your two-minute drill may come unexpectedly, not just late in the game. The most unpredictable aspect of your job search is when an information session or casual encounter turns into an impromptu job interview — and you are suddenly on the spot. You cannot prepare the night before; you must be ready when a person asks:

- Why do you like this field?
- What makes you think you'll succeed in this line of work?
- What experiences, in or out of college, best prepared you for this work?
- What is it about yourself that we would like and could use?

Anyone you meet may be the person who can open the door that you want and need. Every conversation, however informal or casually it may have happened, is a potential job interview. The best way to handle the two-minute-drill scenario is to practice — talk with enough people about yourself, your aspirations, your ideas, and your abilities, that it becomes second nature. Job interviews become like ordinary, informal conversations when you have been through them enough times. Just as football teams execute well in the last two minutes when they have practiced the sequence of plays and are accustomed to the pressure, so will you do well in your "two minutes" when you have been there many times before.

Epilogue

The inspiration for this book was the idea that in college, both athletics and academics are stimulating and worth pursuing with all the commitment a student-athlete can muster. While both require time and energy, we believe that the student-athlete's participation in sports and involvement in schoolwork are mutually beneficial, and not in conflict with each other. The same qualities that make a dedicated athlete are present in productive and satisfied students. In these pages, we have encouraged you most strongly to take courses that will help your personal and career development and to complete your degree because we want you to get everything you deserve from your college education. The life of a student-athlete is not easy, but we hope you'll go the extra mile needed to succeed on the playing field and in the classroom. In the years ahead, you'll be thankful that you did.

Notes

Chapter 1

1. The comment on this page is from Joe Hamelin, a news editor who covered sports, in the *Sacramento Bee* on June 13, 1983.

Chapter 2

1. The quote from Jeff Hembrough was reported in the *New York Times* on December 9, 1981.

2. The quote from Bob Hitch was reported by Paul Desruisseaux in an article entitled "Athletics Deemed a 'Better Citizen' at SMU," published in the *Chronicle of Higher Education* on January 5, 1983.

3. For a horror story involving collegiate basketball and gambling in which suffering was inflicted on guilty and innocent parties, read *Scandals of '51*, by Charles Rosen (New York: Holt, Rinehart and Winston, 1978).

Chapter 3

1. The quote from Oscar Edwards was reported by Michelle Himmelberg in an article entitled "Athlete Traded Skills for Scholarship at Expense of Grades," published in the *Sacramento Bee* on June 9, 1982.

Chapter 4

1. The quote from Tommie Chaiken was found in an article entitled "The Steroids Nightmare," reported by Chaiken and Rick Telander and published in the October 24, 1988, issue of *Sports Illustrated*.

2. The quote from Don Reese was found in an article entitled "I'm Not Worth a Damn," reported by Reese and John Underwood and published in the June 14, 1982, issue of *Sports Illustrated*.

3. The quote from Ken Anderson was reported by William O. Johnson in "What Happened to Our Heroes?" an article that appeared in the August 15, 1983, issue of *Sports Illustrated*.

4. The quote from Cindy Olavarri was found in "Drugs and Redemption," written by C. Koch and published in the April 1989 issue of *Bicycle Guide*.

5. Dr. Kerr stated this opinion on ABC-TV's "Nightline," on March 5, 1985.

6. Robert E. Windsor, M.D., and Daniel Dumitru, M.D., "Anabolic Steroid Use in Athletes," *Post Graduate Medicine* (1988) 84(4):37–49.

7. Dr. Dardick, chairman of the United States Olympic Committee Sports Medicine Committee, stated this opinion on ABC-TV's "Nightline," on March 5, 1985.

8. Mauro G. Pasquale, M.D., *Drug Use and Detection in Amateur Sports* (Ontario: MGD, 1984).

9. Forrest Tennant, M.D., David Black, Ph.D., and Robert O. Voy, M.D., "Anabolic Steroid Dependence with Opioid-Type Features," *New England Journal of Medicine* (September 1986) 1:378.

10. Chaiken and Telander, op. cit.

11. John Hoberman, "Drug Abuse: The Student-Athlete and High-Performance Sport," *The Rules of the Game: Ethics in College Sport,* edited by R. E. Lapchick and J. B. Slaughter (New York: ACE/Macmillan, 1989).

12. Random testing means that many innocent people are tested to catch a few cheaters. The constitutional issue involved centers on invasion of privacy "without probable cause."

13. "Most Athletes Support Drug Testing, Study Shows," *NCAA News* (October 16, 1989).

14. *NCAA News* (August 3, 1988).

15. The quote from Meg Ritchie was reported in an article entitled "Steroids: The Athlete's Opinion," published in the March 1987 issue of *Strength and Conditioning Review.*

16. The quote from Edwin Moses was found in an article entitled "An Athlete's Rx for the Drug Problem," which appeared in the October 10, 1988, issue of *Newsweek.*

17. Michael J. Asken, Ph.D., *Dying to Win* (Washington, D.C.: Acropolis, 1988).

Chapter 5

1. Harry Edwards, "The Single-Minded Pursuit of Sports Fame and Fortune Is Approaching an Institutionalized Triple Tragedy in Black Society," *Ebony* (August 1988).

2. Wilbert Marcellus Leonard II, *A Sociological Perspective of Sport.* 3rd edition. (New York: Macmillan, 1988). According to Leonard, black players also felt more controlled by their coaches than white players did. Leonard's findings were representative of all divisions of college basketball.

3. American Institutes of Research Center for the Study of Athletics, Palo Alto, California, 1989.

4. Ibid.

5. Harry Edwards, "Educating Black Athletes," *Atlantic Monthly* (August 1983).

6. Proposition 48 refers to the NCAA regulation that stipulates that student-athletes who are not academically qualified for admission to a college but who, because of athletic ability, have been accepted anyway, may have to give up athletic competition in their freshman year and

prove that they can do college-level work. Proposition 48 was the name given to the regulation at the time the NCAA voted on it. Its official title in the *NCAA Manual* is Rule 14.3.

7. If you want to avoid Proposition 48 restrictions and want to play as a freshman, you can attend a junior college, a National Association of Intercollegiate Athletics (NAIA) college, or an NCAA Division III college. There is likely to be less pressure at these institutions, but there will still be a lot of time spent in your sport, making it hard for you to catch up academically.

8. The quote by Tharon Mayes was reported in the March 18, 1987, issue of the *NCAA News* and subsequently picked up by the *Hartford Courant.*

9. The quote from Harold Howe II was reported in an article entitled "Harsh Prospects Are Seen for Young Americans Who Do Not Attend College," published in the January 27, 1988, issue of the *Chronicle of Higher Eduction.*

10. The quote from Wilbert Marcellus Leonard II is from a paper entitled "The Sports Experience of the Black College Athlete: Exploitation in the Academy," which he presented in 1989 to the North American Society for the Sociology of Sport.

11. From research conducted by Signithia Fordham in a study of high school students in Washington, D.C. Reported in the *NCAA News* (March 25, 1987).

12. Billy Mills is quoted from a speech he gave at California State University, Sacramento, on March 16, 1988.

13. From a 1989 report on NCAA Division I black athletes by the American Institutes of Research and from a survey by Wilbert Marcellus Leonard II of black athletes at all division levels.

14. John Sherlock, "What Hispanics Are Paid," *USA Today* (August 10, 1989).

15. This quote was acquired in an interview the authors had with the student.

16. Sherlock, op. cit.

17. Michael Wilbon, "One NFL Record That Is Shameful — Minority Hiring," *Sacramento Bee* (February 25, 1990).

18. Al Campanis of the Los Angeles Dodgers and Jimmy "the Greek" Snyder of CBS television were on TV when they voiced their bigoted opinions that not enough people in power believe that blacks can lead teams — both were fired as a result. The authors believe this indicates that people will still act in bigoted ways even though they are not allowed to admit their bigotry publicly.

19. Harry Edwards, "Educating Black Athletes," *Atlantic Monthly* (August 1983).

Chapter 6

1. American Institutes of Research, 1989. The study focuses on male and female NCAA Division I basketball players.

2. K. P. Henschen and D. Fry, "An Archival Study of the Relationship of Intercollegiate Participation and Graduation," *Sociology of Sport Journal* (1984) 1(1):52–56.

3. "NCAA Study of Women Student-Athletes Released," *NCAA News* (August 16, 1989).

4. Craig Neff, "Equality at Last, Part II," *Sports Illustrated* (March 21, 1988).

5. As originally written, Title IX stipulated that if violations were found anywhere at a school, *all* of that school's federal funding was in jeopardy. The Grove City College decision narrowed the penalties to only those programs at the school that were violating the law. School-wide liability was restored by the Civil Rights Restoration Act of 1988.

6. Neff, op. cit.

7. "Net Receipts Top $1 Million in Women's Basketball," *NCAA News* (July 19, 1989).

8. Elaine Blinde, "Intrinsic Motivation and the Female Intercollegiate Athlete," a paper presented at a meeting of the North American Society for the Sociology of Sport in Las Vegas, Nevada, in 1988.

9. Debbie Ryan is quoted from "Big Jump in Money and Prestige Spurs Cheating in Women's Basketball, Coaches and Players Say," an article written by Charles S. Farrell and published in the January 29, 1986, issue of the *Chronicle of Higher Education*.

10. "Eastern Kentucky Women's Basketball Placed on Probation," *NCAA News* (August 2, 1989).

11. The quote from Robert Rossi was found in "Female Basketball Players Outperform Their Male Counterparts in the Classroom," an article by Douglas Lederman that appeared in the August 16, 1989, issue of the *Chronicle of Higher Education*.

12. Vivian Acosta and L. J. Carpenter, "Perceived Causes of the Declining Representation of Women Leaders in Intercollegiate Sports — 1988 Update," *NAPEHE Action Line* (1989) 12(1):8–10.

13. C. Potera and M. Kort, "Are Women Coaches an Endangered Species?" *Women's Sports and Fitness* (1986) 8(9).

14. Acosta and Carpenter, op. cit.

15. The quote by E. C. Frederick was found in "Women Eventually Could Equal Men in Sport, Researcher Says," an article in the April 6, 1988, issue of the *NCAA News*.

16. R. A. Carey, "Physiological Aspects of Women and Exercise," *Exercise Medicine: Physiological Principles and Clinical Applications*, edited by A. A. Bove and D. T. Lowenthal (North Carolina: Academy Press, 1983).

17. C. L. Wells, *Women, Sport, and Performance: A Physiological Perspective* (Champaign, Ill.: Human Kinetics, 1985).

18. M. E. Duquin, "Perceptions of Sport: A Study in Sexual Attraction"; "Sex Roles and Achievement," *Psychology of Motor Behavior and Sport,* edited by D. M. Landers and R. W. Christina (Champaign, Ill.: Human Kinetics, 1977).

19. Sexual advances between female coaches and male athletes are rare in part because women coaching men at the collegiate level is a rarity.

20. From the 1989 Women's International Tennis Association Media Guide.

Chapter 7

1. Bob Dart, "Redskins Star Weeps, Admits He Can't Read," *Sacramento Bee* (May 19, 1989).

2. Jack Curry, "Through Lawsuit Kevin Ross May Make His Point," *Sacramento Bee* (February 11, 1990).

3. The quote from Dan Offenburger was reported by Edward Menaker in the October 3, 1982, issue of the *New York Times.*

4. Ted Gup, "Foul!" *Time* (April 3, 1989).

5. The quote from Grant Darkow was reported in the December 9, 1981, issue of the *New York Times.*

6. Gup, op. cit.

Chapter 8

1. Bear Bryant was quoted by James Michener in *Sports in America* (New York: Random House, 1976).

2. A complete list of the skills students need to do college-level work can be found in the booklet *Academic Preparation for College: What Students Need to Know and Be Able to Do* (New York: The College Board, 1983).

Chapter 9

1. The passage that opens this chapter is from an article written by Tony Kornheiser for the *Washington Post* and reprinted in the Harrisburg *Patriot-News,* May 16, 1982.

2. The quote from the former college athlete was reported by N. Scott Vance in "Life After Sport Found Difficult for Ex-athletes," published in the November 11, 1982, issue of the *Chronicle of Higher Education.*

3. Samuel H. Armacost spoke at the University of California at Berkeley's School of Business commencement in 1983.

Chapter 10

1. The quote from Ferdi Taygan was reported by Donna Doherty in an article entitled "Starting Over: Is There Life After Pro Tennis?" which appeared in the December 1981 issue of *Tennis Magazine*.

2. The professional associations listed in this section were identified in the *Encyclopedia of Associations, 1988,* 22nd ed., edited by Karin E. Koek and Susan Boyles Martin (Detroit: Gale Research Company, 1988).

Chapter 11

1. The quote from a senior vice president of the First Atlanta Corporation was reported in "The Money Chase," which appeared in *Time* on May 4, 1981.